Denton Jaques Snider

Homer in Chios

An Epopee

Denton Jaques Snider

Homer in Chios
An Epopee

ISBN/EAN: 9783744670432

Printed in Europe, USA, Canada, Australia, Japan

Cover: Foto ©ninafisch / pixelio.de

More available books at **www.hansebooks.com**

HOMER IN CHIOS.

An Epopee

BY

DENTON J. SNIDER.

ST. LOUIS.
SIGMA PUBLISHING CO.,
210 PINE STREET,
1891.

CONTENTS.

I. MNEMOSYNE.
   The Making of the Poet. 5
II. CALLIOPE.
   The Call of the Muse. 27
III. EUTERPE.
   The Daughter of Homer. 47
IV. ERATO.
   The Stranger of Northland. . . . 63
V. CLIO.
   The Travels of Homer. 85
VI. TERPSICHORE.
   The Pedagogue Chian. 113
VII. MELPOMENE.
   The Singer of Ascra. 131
VIII. THALIA.
   The Songstress of Lesbos. 149
IX. POLYHYMNIA.
   The Psalmist of Israel. 173
X. URANIA.
   The Marriage. 201

I.

Mnemosyne.

The Making of The Poet.

ARGUMENT.

HOMER, the poet, having returned in old age to Chios, his birth-place, an island not far from the coast of Asia Minor, tells the story of his early life to his pupils. Two chief influences wrought upon his childhood. The first was that of the smith, Chalcon, who was both artisan and artist — both vocations in early times were united in one man — and who revealed to the budding poet the forms of the Gods. The second influence was that of his mother, Crethéis (name given by Herodotus, Vita Hom). She was the depository of fable and folk-lore, which she told to her boy in the spirit of a poet, and which are the chief materials of his two great poems. So Homer reaches back to his earliest years by the aid of Mnemósyne (memory), who according to Hesiod (Theogon. 915) was the mother of the Nine Muses.

"Fair was the day when I first peeped into the
  workshop of Chalcon,
Chalcon, the smith, who wrought long ago in the
  city of Chios;
Now that day is the dawn of my life, which I yet
  can remember,
All my hours run back to its joy as my very beginning,
And one beautiful moment then let in the light
  of existence,
Starting within me the strain that thrills through
  my days to this minute!
Still the old flash I can see as I peeped at the
  door of the workshop,
Memory whispers the tale of the rise of a world
  that I saw there
Memory, muse of the past, is whispering faintly
  the story.

Chalcon the smith, far-famed in the sun-born
    island of Chios,
Stood like a giant and pounded the bronze in the
    smoke of his smithy,
Pounded the iron until it would sing in a tune
    with the anvil,
Sing in a tune with the tongs and the anvil and
    hammer together,
Making the music of work that rang to the ends
    of the city.
Figures he forced from his soul into metal, most
    beautiful figures,
Forced them by fury of fire beneath cunning
    strokes of the hammer;
As he thought them, he wrought them to loveliest
    forms of the living,
Wrought them to worshipful shapes of the Gods,
    who dwell on Olympus.
That was when I was still but a child in the home
    of my mother,
Sole dear home of my life, the home of Cretheis
    my mother!
Only two doors from his shop with its soot stood
    her clean little cottage,
Vainly she strove to restrain her clean little boy
    from the smithy,
But he would slip out the house and away, as
    soon as she washed him,
Off and away to the forge just where the smutch
    was the deepest.

How I loved the great bellows puffing its breath on the charcoal!
And the storm of the sparkles that lit up the smithy with starlight!
And the hiss of the iron red-hot when thrust into water!
Greatest man in the world I deemed at that time to be Chalcon,
And his smithy to me rose up a second Olympus,
Where the Gods and the Heroes I saw move forth into being;
Him too deemed I divine, like Hephæstus, a God in his workshop.
As he thought, so he wrought — he pounded and rounded the metal
Till it breathed and would move of itself to a corner and stand there,
Till it spoke, and speaking would point up beyond to Immortals.
Bare to the waist and shaggy the breast of the big-boned Chalcon,
As it heaved with an earthquake of joy in the shock of creation;
Thick were the thews of his arm and balled at each blow till his shoulder,
At the turn of his wrist great chords swelled out on his fore-arm,
One huge hand clasped the grip of the tongs in its broad bony knuckles,

Th'other clutched hold of the sledge and whirled
 it around by the handle;
Shutting his jaws like a lion, and grating his
 teeth in his fury,
Whirled he the ponderous sledge to hit in the
 heat of the iron;
While the veins underneath would heave up the
 grime on his forehead,
Smote he the might of the metal with all the grit
 of a Titan;
Working mid flashes of flame that leaped out the
 belly of darkness,
Smote he and sang he a song in response to the
 song of his hammer."

So spake aged Homerus, the bard, as he sat in
 his settle,
Where grew a garden of fruit, the fig and the
 pear and the citron,
Grapes suspended in clusters and trees of the
 luscious pomegranate.
He had returned to his home with a life full of
 light and of learning;
Wandering over the world, he knew each country
 and city,
Man he had seen in the thought and the deed, the
 Gods he had seen too;
Home he had reached once more, the violet
 island of Chios,
Blind, ah blind, but with sight in his soul and a
 sun in his spirit.

THE MAKING OF THE POET.

Youths were standing around him and hearkened
    to what he was telling,
Bright-eyed youths, who had come to his knees
    from each region of Hellas,
Homerids hopeful of song, the sons of the genius
    of Homer,
By the new tale of Troy inspired, they sought to
    make measures,
Striving to learn of the master to wield the
    hexameter mighty,
As high Zeus the thunderbolt wields in a flash
    through the Heavens,
Leaping from cloud unto cloud and leaving long
    lines of its splendor,
Rolling the earth in its garment of resonant
    reverberation.
Luminous too was the look of the boys, lit up
    by the Muses,
Eager they turned to the sage, and begged for
    the rest of his story;
Soon into musical words he began again spinning
    his life-thread:

"Chalcon, the smith, was the maker of Gods
    in the smoke of his smithy!
Out of darkness he wrought them, out of chaos
    primeval,
Striking great blows that lit up the night with
    the sparks of creation

Which would flash from his mind into metal
through strokes of the hammer.
Aye, and the maker of me in his Gods he was
also — that Chalcon;
He perchance did not know it — the world he
was mightily making.
All the Graces he wrought into shape, and loved
as he wrought them,
And the Fates he could form in his need, though
he never did love them,
But the snake-tressed Furies he banished in hate
from his workshop.
I could always forecast what he wrought and
whether it went well,
Whether full freely the thought ran out of his
soul to the matter,
For he would sing at his work an old Prome-
thean ditty.
Tuneful, far-hinting it poured from his soul into
forms of his God-world,
Strong deep notes which seemed to direct each
sweep of the hammer,
Just at the point where a stroke might finish the
work of the master,
Or a blow ill-struck might shatter a year of his
labor.
Then bright notes would well from within as he
filed and he chiseled,
Seeking to catch and to hold in a shape the
gleam of his genius.

Battles he pictured in silver and gold on the
shield of the warrior,
Corselets he plaited in proof and swords he
forged for the Hero,
Many a goblet he made wreathed round with the
frolic of Bacchus,
All the Gods he could fashion to life, in repose
and in motion,
Their high shapes he could call from his soul, together and singly,
Call with their godhood down from the heights of
the radiant Heavens,
Till the dingy old smithy shot into Olympian
sunshine.
Chalcon, Oh Chalcon, me thou hast formed in
forming Immortals,
And the song of thy hammer I hear in the ring
of my measures,
Oft I can feel thee striking thy anvil still in my
heart-strokes,
Which are forging my strains like thee when thou
smotest the metal,
Till it rang and it sang the strong tune of the
stress of thy labor.
Chalcon, thy workshop went with me in every
turn of my travel,
Through the East and the West of wide Hellas,
through island and mainland,
Through the seas in the storm, through mountains rolling in thunder,

With me it went in my wandering, e'en to the
    top of Olympus:
Never thy shapes shall fade from the sight of my
    soul, Oh Chalcon."

  Quickly the poet turned round in his seat and
    said to his servant:
" Come, Amyntas my boy, now bring some wine
    in my goblet,
Chian wine in my goblet wrought by the cunning
    of Chalcon,
Which he gave to me once when I sang him my
    earliest measures,
Round which are dancing the youths at the tast-
    ing the must of the wine-press,
While the God overgrown with leaves and with
    vines looks laughing;
Chalcon gave it me once as a prize when I sang
    in his workshop,
Sang him my earliest measures in tune to the
    strokes of his hammer."

  Beardless Amyntas, the cup bearer, brought the
    chalice of Chian,
Choicest of wine, that sparkled and danced on
    the rim of the chalice,
Draught of the sea, and the earth, and the sun-
    shine together commingled,
Liquid poesy, stealthily sung in each drop by the
    wine-god.

THE MAKING OF THE POET.

Softly the singer sipped off the glittering beads
  of the beaker,
Touching his lip to the line where the rim and
  the brim come together,
Where flash twinkles of joy and laugh in the eye
  of the drinker.
That was the essence of Chios distilled from
  the heart of her mountains,
Tempered hot in the fires that smoulder still in
  the soil there,
Drawn by the grape into drops that shoot into
  millions of sparkles,
Generous vintage of Chios, renewing the heart of
  the singer.

When his thirst he had slaked and his thought
  had returned to his thinking,
Sweetly he lowered his voice to the note of a musical whisper,
And he bent forward his body as if he were
  telling a secret:
"Once, I remember, Chalcon was making a group
  of the Muses,
Sacred givers of song, to be borne to a festival
  splendid,
Where each singer had in their presence to
  sing for the laurel.
What do you think he did as I stood with him
  there in the smithy?

Me he turned into bronze, and put me among the Nine Sisters,
As if I their young brother might be, their one only brother;
In the center he placed me, aye in the heart of the Muses,
Sweet Calliope kissed me there in the workshop of Chalcon,
Even in bronze I could feel her embrace on that day — I now feel it —
And I could hear her soft breathings that told of the deeds of the Heroes.
Still I can feel, e'en though I be old, the kiss of the Muses,
And at once I respond to their music in words of my measures,
Yielding my heart and my voice to their promptings and gentle persuasion.
O good Chalcon, memory keeps thee alive, as I love thee!
Keeps thee working in me as the maker who is the poet;
Ever living thou art in thy glorious shapes of Immortals,
Though thou, a mortal by Fate, hast gone to the Houses of Hades,
Whither I too must soon go — the call I can hear from the distance,
I too a mortal by Fate must pass to the shades of my Heroes."

THE MAKING OF THE POET.

There he paused on the tremulous thought of a
  hope and a sorrow,
And the sweet word died away on his lips thrown
  far in the future.
Hark! the voice of a song creeps into the house
  of Homerus,
Filling his home with love and with life to the
  measure of music,
Fresh from the youth of the heart, the fountain
  of hope everlasting.
Though unseen the sweet singer, hidden in
  leaves of an arbor,
All the youths well knew who it was, and stood
  for a moment,
Bating the breath and bending the head to listen
  the better,
And to quaff each note to the full, for the voice
  that was singing
Poured out the soul of a maiden, the beautiful
  daughter of Homer,
Whom those boys were more eager to hear than
  to study their verses,
Aye, more eager to hear the daughter than
  hearken the father.

He, when the strain had ceased, with a sigh
  broke into the silence:
"Ah! the fleet years! how like is that note to
  the note of my mother,

As she hymned to her work or sang me to sleep
    on her pallet!
Early my father had died, his face I no longer
    remember,
But the voice which speaks when I speak from
    my heart is always —
Well do I know it — the voice of my mother,
    Cretheis my mother!"

  Overmastered a moment by tears, he soon
    overmastered
All of the weaker man in himself, and thus he
    proceeded:
" I was telling the tale of the wonderful work-
    shop of Chalcon,
Where I saw all the deities rise into form in
    a rapture,
Coming along with their sunshine to stand in the
    soot of the smithy,
Happy Olympian Gods who once fought and put
    down the dark Titans.
Bearing their spell in my soul, I always went
    home to my mother,
And I would beg her to tell me who were the
    Gods and the Muses,
All this beautiful folk whom Chalcon had brought
    from the summits,
From free sunny Olympus down into the smoth-
    ering smithy.

THE MAKING OF THE POET.

She would begin with a glow in her eyes and tell
me their story,
Meanwhile plying the distaff — she never could
help being busy —
All of their tales she knew, by the hundreds and
hundreds she knew them,
Tales of the beings divine, once told of their
dealings with mankind,
When they came to our earth and visibly mingled
with mortals.
New was always the word on the tongue of
Crethéis my mother,
Though she dozens of times before had told the
same story,
Still repeating when I would call for it, ever re-
peating,
For a good tale, like the sun, doth shine one day
as the other.
What a spell on her lip when up from her lap I
was looking,
Watching her mouth in its motion, whence drop-
ped those wonderful stories!
Oft I thought I could pick up her word in my
hand as it fell there,
Keep it and carry it off, for my play a most beau-
tiful plaything,
Which I could toss on the air when I chose, like
a ball or an apple,
Catch it again as it fell in its flight, for the word
was a thing then.

Mark! what I as a child picked up, the old man
    still plays with:
Words made of breath, but laden with thought
    more solid than granite,
Pictures of heroes in sound that lasts, when
    spoken, forever,
Images fair of the world and marvelous legends
    aforetime,
All of them living in me as they fell from the
    lips of my mother."

  There he stopped for a moment and passed his
    hand to his forehead,
As if urging Mnemosyne now for the rest of
    the story;
Soon came the Muse to the aid of the poet, and
    thus he continued:
" How she loved the songs of old Hellas, and
    loved all its fabling!
Well she could fable herself and color her speech
    with her heart-beats.
I have known her to make up a myth which
    spread through all Chios,
Thence to island and mainland wherever Hellenic
    is spoken.
Once I heard far out by the West in a town of
    Zakynthus,
At a festival one of her lays, which I knew in
    my cradle,

Sung by the bard of the town as his guerdon of
  song from the Muses.
And now let me confess, too, my debt, the debt
  of my genius!
Many a flash of the fancy is hers which you read
  in my poems,
Many a roll of the rhythm, and many a turn of
  the language,
Many a joy she has given, and many a tear she
  has dropped there,
Merciful sighs at the stroke of grim Fate on the
  back of the mortal —
All are remembrances fallen to me from the lips
  of my mother."

For a moment he ceased, till he gathered his
  voice into firmness,
Smoothing the tremulous trill that welled from
  his heart into wavelets,
Smoothing and soothing the quivering thoughts
  which Memory brought him:
"Hard was her lot, she had to work daily
  through Chios by spinning,
For herself and her boy she fought the rough
  foes of existence,
Making her living by toil that flew from the tips
  of her fingers,
Deft and swift in the cunning which gives all
  its worth unto labor.

Yet more cunning she showed in spinning the
  threads of a story
Till they all came together forming a garment of
  beauty,
Than in twirling the distaff and reeling the yarn
  from the spindle.
But she too, my poor mother, was laid in the
  earth, as was fated,
For the Fates span out the frail thread of her
  life at their pleasure."

Here again the old man made a stop with a
  gaze in his features
As if prying beyond to behold the unspeakable
  secret;
But he came back to himself with a joy in his
  look and continued:
" It was she who gave me the love and the lore
  of the legend,
Training my youth to her song which throbbed
  to the best of the ages —
All the great men of the Past and great women,
  the mothers of Heroes.
Do you know it was she who first told me the
  story of Thetis —
Thetis the Goddess-Mother, whose son was the
  Hero Achilles?
Tenderly told she the tale of the boy who was
  born to do great things,

Who from his birth had in him the spark divine
of his mother,
Though he had to endure all the sorrow of being
a hero,
Suffer the pang that goes with the gift of the
Gods to a mortal.
Then in a frenzy of hope she would clasp me
unto her bosom,
Dreaming the rest of her dream in the soft in-
spiration of silence,
Yet you could see what it was by the light that
was lit in her presence,
See it all by the light of her soul that shone from
her visage.
Once in her joy she arose with her arms out-
stretched mid her story,
Showing how Thetis arose from the deeps in a
cloud o'er the billow,
That she, the Goddess, might secretly take her
son to her bosom,
To impart what was best of herself — the godlike
endurance —
And to arouse in him too the new valor to meet
the great trial.
O fond soul of my mother, how well that day
I remember,
When thou toldest the tale of the bees that flew
to my cradle,
Dropping out of the skies on a sudden along with
the sunbeams,

Humming and buzzing through all of the house
    as if they were swarming,
Till they lit on my lips as I slept but never once
    stung me,
Never stung thee, though running around in thy
    fright to defend me,
Smiting and slashing with stick or with rag or
    whatever came handy,
Scorching at last their leathery wings with their
    own waxen tapers!
But ere they flew, in spite of the fire and fight of
    the household,
They had left on my lips their cells of the clear-
    flowing honey,
Honey clear-flowing and sweet, though bitter the
    struggle to give it;
Even the bees had to pay for giving the gift of
    their sweetness.

  Then wert thou happy, Cretheis, then wert thou
    sad too, my mother,
Pensive, forethinking afar on what the God had
    intended,
Who had sent the dumb bee to speak as a sign
    unto mortals.
What thy son was to do and endure flashed into
    thy vision,
Double that flash of the future, joyful, sorrow-
    ful also,

And thou didst say to thyself and the God, bending over to kiss me:
'Let it fall — the lot of his life; I feel what is coming:
He must distil from the earth into speech all the sweetness of living,
He must pour from his heart into song all the nectar of sorrow;
Let it fall — the lot of his life; though hard be the trial,
Always there will be left on his lips the hive of its honey.'"

II.

Calliope.

The Call of The Muse.

ARGUMENT.

Homer now tells the third chief influence which helped make him a poet. This influence was the bard of the town, Ariston, who sang on the borderland between East and West, but was not able to sing of the great conflict between Troy and Greece. It was Ariston who suggested this theme to Homer, and bade the youth go out to the sea-shore, where was the cave of the Muses, and listen to the voice which would speak to him there. Calliope, the epic Muse, appears to him, tells him what he must do and suffer, and inspires him with his great vocation. He goes home to his mother and tells her what the Muse has said to him; his mother after a short internal struggle, bids him go at once and follow the call of the Muse.

Thus to the whisper of fleeting Mnemosyne,
mother of Muses,
Homer was yielding his heart and shaping her
shadowy figures.
While he was speaking, rose up the roar of the
sea in the distance,
Which an undertone gave to his measures, mighty,
majestic,
Wreathing the roll of its rhythm in words of the
tale he was telling,
Giving the musical stroke of its waves to the
shore of the island,
Giving the stroke for the song to the beautiful
island of Chios.
All the sea was a speech, and spoke in the language of Homer,

Aye, the Ægean spoke Greek, and sang the refrain of great waters,
All the billows were singing that day hexameters rolling,
Rolling afar from the infinite sea to the garden of Homer.

   Stopped in the stretch of his thought the poet lay back in his settle,
Seemingly lost in the maze where speech fades out into feeling;
He was silent awhile, though not at the end of his story.
Aged and blind he was now, recalling the days of his boyhood,
When he saw all the world of fair forms, as it rose up in Hellas,
Rise from the hand of the smith and rise from the lips of his mother,
Saw too himself in the change of the years becoming the singer.

   Soon spake a youth at his side, it was the best of his pupils,
Called Demodocus, son of Demodocus, Ithacan rhapsode,
Who belonged to an ancestry born into song from old ages:
"Did you have no bard of the village, no teacher of measures,

Who could melt the rude voice of the people to
    rhythm of music?
Men of that strain we have in our Ithaca, they
    are my clansmen.
Still I follow the craft, and to thee, best singer,
    I come now,
That I be better than they, far better in song
    than my fathers."

Here he suddenly stopped and glanced out into
    the garden,
For there flitted an airy form of a maid in the
    distance,
Going and coming amid the flowers — the
    daughter of Homer,
Whom Demodocus loved and sought as the meed
    of his merit,
He would carry away not only the verse of the
    master,
But would take, in the sweep of his genius, also
    the daughter.
Yet the maiden held off, declaring the youth was
    conceited.

But the father in words of delight replied to
    his scholar:
" Well bethought! a good learner! thou thinkest
    ahead of the teacher!
Just of the bard I was going to speak, he rose in
    my mind's eye

Suddenly with thy question — the face and the
 form of Ariston.
Every day I went to the place of the market to
 hear him —
Deep-toned Ariston, the singer of praises to Gods
 and to Heroes,
Chanting the fray and the valorous deed in the
 ages aforetime,
While the crowd stood around in reverent silence and listened.
He was the bard of the town, he knew what had
 been and will be,
Knew the decree of Zeus and could read it out of
 the Heavens,
Knew too, the heart of man, and could tell every
 thought in its throbbing.
At the festivals sang he through all of the ham-
 lets of Chios,
He was the voice of the isle, the mythical hoard
 of old treasures;
Song and story and fable, even the jest and the
 riddle —
All were his charge and his choice, by the care
 and the call of the Muses.
High beat his heart as he poured out its music
 singing of Heroes,
Every word of his voice was a tremulous pulse-
 beat of Hellas,
Doomful the struggle he saw in the land and fateful its Great Men.

Often he sang the sad lot of Bellerophon, hero
  of Argos,
Who once crossed to the Orient, leaving the
  mainland of Europe,
Quitting his home in the West for the charm of
  a Lycian maiden,
Daughter fair of the king who dwelt by the eddying Xanthus.
Many a demon he slew, destroying the shapes of
  the ugly,
Savages tamed he to beautiful law, and the law,
  too, of beauty,
Monsters, Chimeras, wild men and wild women
  he brought to Greek order,
Amazons haters of husbands, and Solymi mount-
  aineers shaggy.
But the Hero, for such is his fate, sank to what
  he subjected,
In the success of his deed he lapsed and fell under
  judgment,
Hateful to Gods is success, though much it is
  loved by us mortals,
Victory is the trial, most hard in the end to the
  victor.

Such was the strain of Ariston, here on the
  borderland singing
Where two continents stand and look with a scowl
  at each other
Over the islanded waters, ready to smite in the
  struggle.

Every Greek in our Chios then heard Bellero-
    phon's echo,
Heard in the deep-sounding name of the Hero an
    echo that thrilled him,
Felt in his bosom the reverberation of Bellero-
    phontes,
For he could find in himself the same peril of
    lapsing from Hellas,
Sinking to Asia back from the march of the world
    to the westward."

Sympathy touched in its tenderest tone the
    voice of Homerus,
As his words sank down at the end of the line to
    a whisper,
Then to a silence, the silence of thought, which
    spoke from his presence.
What was the matter with Homer, and why that
    shadow in sunshine?
Did he find in his own Greek soul a gleam of the
    danger?
Did his poetical heart then enter the trance of
    temptation?
He must respond to the passion, aye to the guilt,
    in his rapture,
He must glow with the deed of the Hero, even
    the wrongful,
Never forgetting the law, and sternly pronounc-
    ing the judgment.

Soon he rallied and rose, and his voice returned
  with his story:
" Well I knew the old man and eagerly stored up
  his treasures,
Aged Ariston loved me, and made me his daily
  companion,
I was his scholar, perchance, as ye are now in my
  training.
Once in a mutual moment of freedom I ventured
  to ask him:
' O my Ariston, sing me to-day the new song
  of our nation,
Born of the deed, the last great deed we have all
  done together,
All the Hellenes have done it, methinks, in the
  might of one impulse,
Fighting our destiny's fight to possess and pre-
  serve the new future,
Saving the beautiful woman and saving ourselves
  in her safety;
That is the deed of Troy and its lay of the Hero
  Achilles!
Seek not so far for an action when near in thy
  way is the greatest.'

Thus I spake, and his face on the spot turned
  into a battle.
'Ah!' he replied 'too near me it lies, just
  that is the hindrance!

I must leave it behind to another, for I cannot
 touch it;
Still my heart is cleft by that terrible struggle
 asunder,
Wounded I was in the strife, remediless still I am
 bleeding,
Cureless I feel it to be — that wound of the
 Greeks and the Trojans!
I was on both sides during the war, and yet upon
 neither,
Standing aloof from each, yet standing with one
 and the other,
With father Priam of Troy as well as with Greek
 Agamemnon —
Tossed to this part or that, and torn into shreds
 by the Furies;
Greeks had my brain on their side, the Trojans
 had hold of my heart-strings;
With that breach in my soul, how could I make
 any music?
I cannot stand the stress, the horrible stress of
 the struggle
Always renewed in my song whose every word is
 a blood-stain.
But hereafter the man will arise who is able to
 sing it,
Healing the wound in himself and the time,
 which in me is unhealing;
One shall come and sing of that mightiest deed
 of the Argives,

He shall arise, the poet of Hellas — the man hath
 arisen
Who will take it and mould it and make it the
 song of the ages.
Youth, be thou singer of Troy and the war for
 the beautiful Helen,
Sing of the Hero in wrath, and reconciled sing
 of the Hero!'

Thus spoke Ariston the bard; what a life he
 started within me!
Chaos I was, but the sun of a song had smitten
 the darkness,
And my soul bore a universe, with one word as a
 midwife,
That was the word of the poet, who spoke as
 the maker primeval,
Calling the sun and the earth from the void, and
 the firmament starry.
Always welfare he brought to the people who
 hearkened his wisdom,
And he was ever alive with the thought of bringing a blessing,
Climbing the height of the highest Gods, where
 dwells freedom from envy.
After deep silence, the mother of good, he sol-
 emnly added:

'Now is the moment to seek the divinity's
 sign for thy calling,

Godlike the token must be, for of Gods is the
    breath of the singer;
Go to the grot of the sweet-voiced Muses down
    by the sea-side
Where old Nereus scooped out of stone his son-
    orous cavern,
Sounding the strains of a lyre that is played by
    the hands of great waters,
As they incessantly strike on the sands and the
    shells and the rock walls,
Reaching out from the heart of the sea for a
    stroke of their fingers,
Just for one stroke of their billowy fingers, then
    broken forever,
Playing the notes of a song that can only be
    heard by a poet.
There thou wilt hear, if it also be thine, the voice
    of the Muses,
Who will give thee their golden word and the
    high consecration;
But if it be not within thee already, they will be
    silent,
Silence is the command of the God to seek them
    no further;
Then thou wilt hear in their house by the sea but
    a roar and a rumble,
But a roar and a rumble of godless waters in
    discord;
Wheel about in thy tracks, perchance thou wilt
    make a good cobbler.'

Not yet cold was the word when I started and
    came to the cavern,
Set with many a glistening gem overhead in the
    ceiling,
Decked with sculpture of stone cut out on its
    sides by the Naiads,
Making a gallery fair of the forms of the Gods
    of the waters,
Round whose feet mid the tangle and fern were
    playing the mermaids,
Smiting the wine-dark deep, as they dived from
    the sight of the sea-boys,
Smiting the blue-lit billows above into millions
    of sparkles,
Into millions of cressets that lit up the cavern
    like starlight,
Secret cavern of love for the nymphs, the watery
    dwellers,
Echoing music afar of the kiss of the earth and
    the ocean.
Well I knew the recess for often before I had
    been there,
Oft I had heard the report that told of the sil-
    very swimmers,
Told of the maidens and youths who loved far
    under the billows,
Loved one another far under the billows and sang
    the sweet love song,
Swimming around in the grots and the groves of
    deep Amphitrite,

Or reclining to rest on the couch of the pearl or
    the coral.
  There I had seen in the sunset the car of hoary
    Poseidon,
Skimming across the wave with his train to his
    watery temple
Over the golden bridge of the sunbeams that lay
    on the ripples,
Bridge that lay on the ripples ablaze in the sheen
    of Apollo,
Spanning the stretch of the sea from Chios away
    to the sundown.
  There I had seen old Proteus, changeful God of
    the waters,
Forming, transforming himself, the one, into
    shapes of all being,
Into the leaf-shaking tree and into the shaggy-
    maned lion,
Creeping reptile, blazing fire, and flowing water;
Still I saw him, the one and the same, under-
    neath all his changes.
  There I had seen the beautiful Nereid, daugh-
    ter of Nereus,
Chased by the sinuous Triton, the man of the sea
    in his passion,
Who would snort in his fury whenever the mer-
    maid escaped him,
Spouting the foam of his rage up into the face
    of the heavens,

Rising and shaking his billowy curls and blowing
his sea-horn.

There I lay down on a pallet of stone and slid
into slumber,
While I was sleeping, stood up before me a troop
of fair women,
Nine of them, sisters who sang in a circle, they
were the Muses,
Singing along with their mother, Mnemosyne,
who was the tenth one,
Who would always give them the hint of the
matter and music,
Looking backward she gave to the Muses the
beat of the present.
Soon they arose into beautiful shapes from the
strains of the cavern,
Quite as once I had seen them arise in the
smithy of Chalcon,
Taking divinity's form in the strokes of his
dexterous hammer.
One of them stepped from the group, alto-
gether the tallest and fairest,
And she kissed me; it was Calliope who in the
cavern
Gave me again the sweet kiss that I felt in
the smoke of the smithy;
But her lips began moving with words in the
twilight of dreamland,

And with a smile she stretched out her hand and
    spake me her message:
  'Hail, O son of Cretheis, doubly the son of thy
    mother,
Son of her mythical soul and son of her beautiful
    body,
Hearken, dear youth, to our call, for thou hast
    been chosen the master,
Thee we endow with all of our gifts of speech
    and of spirit,
But take heed of the warning, henceforth be ready
    to suffer;
Mark it! along with each gift the Gods have a
    penalty given,
For each good that they grant unto mortals,
    strict is the payment;
Not without toil is the gift of the Muses, not
    without sorrow;
Nay, a Fury is thine, called Sympathy, rending
    thy bosom,
Making the fate of the human thine own in the
    song which thou singest;
Into the stroke of thy heart we have put each
    pang of the mortal,
Which will throb and respond in a strain to the
    cry of the victim;
Answer thou must in agony every twinge of his
    torture,
Pass through his sorrow of soul, and leap with
    the sting of his body;

And when he goes down to death, thou living
 must go along with him,
Go to the uttermost region beyond the line of
 the sunset,
Living descend to the dead and speak in the
 Houses of Hades.
 Now thou must wander; thy path runs over
  each mountain of Hellas,
Over the river and plain to the site of each ham-
 let and city,
That thou see all its people and hear them tell
 their own story;
Not till then art thou fitted to sing the great song
 of Achæa.
First to Troy thou must pass and look at the
 plain and the ruins,
Thou wilt hear on the air the fierce clangor of
 arms in the onset,
Hear the groans of the wounded, the shouts of
 the victor and vanquished,
Hear the voice of the graves by the shore of the
 blue Hellespontus.
Still the ghosts of the dead are fighting, will fight
 there forever!
Catch the fleet flight of their words in thy strain,
 in its adamant fix them,
Make adamantine the speech of the spectres by
 rolling Scamander.
Also the Gods thou must see descending from
 lofty Olympus,

Aiding one side or the other, inspiring this hero
    or that one,
Nay, they must fight on Olympus, the Gods
    must have too a battle,
But forget not omnipotence — high above all of
    them Zeus sits.
'Tis our vision we grant thee, to spy out their
    forms in the ether,
As they flit hither a thought of the mortal, but
    yet a God too!'

    Loftily spoke the grand Muse, when she
    changed to a look of compassion,
Which made me weep for myself as again she
    began to forecast me:
' O, the hard law which for good the divine must
    lay on the human!
For thy vision celestial the penalty too must be
    given,
In return for the boon thou must yield thy ter-
    restrial vision,
Sight at last in old age will be weighed and be
    paid for thy insight.
Poverty thou must endure on the way for the
    cause of thy poem,
Thine is to hunger in body and thine to suffer in
    spirit,
Still kind hands will reach thee a morsel where-
    ever thou singest,

Kindred souls will speak thee a word of sweet
  recognition,
Then go further and sing, though at first nobody
  may listen,
Further and further and sing till the end has been
  sung of thy journey.
Hard is thy lot, I warn thee — the lot of the
  God-gifted singer,
But it cannot be shunned — to shun it were
  death without dying.
Go now, get thee ready at once, and set out on
  thy travels.'

Roused by the voice of command I awoke in a
  swirl of the senses,
Homeward I hastened, reflecting how I might
  break to my mother
What I had heard in a swound from the Muses
  so fateful, foretelling
Sad departure, ordaining divinely the long sep-
  aration.
Great was her joy at the marvelous tale, and
  great was her sorrow,
Tear was fighting with tear in a war of delight
  and of anguish,
Till in the masterful might of her heart she rose
  up and bade me:
' Go my son, start to-day, thou must follow the
  call of the Muses,

Suffer whatever of weal and of woe the Goddesses
   give thee;
Thou wast the hope of my life, but gladly I shall
   thee surrender,
Follow the call of the Muses, I can still spin for
   a living.' "

III.

Euterpe.

The Daughter of Homer.

ARGUMENT.

While Homer is telling to the youths the story of his early life, his daughter Praxilla, who has hitherto been kept in the background, appears and begs that she be allowed to share in the school and in the gifts of her father. She refuses all the allurements of love till this right be accorded her. Homer grants her petition, and finds in her words a strong note plainly indicating the future. Then they all move to the shrine of Apollo, and the poet prays the God for light within, and also prays for the God, who is still to unfold.

Strong and firm yet tender in tone had spoken
   Homerus,
Ever the son of his mother and born each day of
   her spirit,
Merely the thought of her brought back the sight
   to his eyes, though he saw not,
And to his vision, though shut to the world, her
   shape had arisen,
Speaking the long and the last farewell as he left
   her to travel,
Speaking the words which Memory, shyest of
   Muses, had whispered.

Of a sudden he stopped, borne off by the tide
   of his feelings,
Out of the region of speech, which died like a
   beautiful music

Far on the hills, with echoes repeating themselves on his heart-strings,
As he hearkened that voice which can only be heard in its silence.
Always the poet responds to the lightest touch of his poem,
In it the music he hears, and also the music beyond it,
For two strains his measures must have, both singing together,
One of mortals and earth, the other of Gods and Olympus,
One of gloom and of fate, the other of light and of freedom.
Priest though he be at the altar of song, he is also the victim,
And he yields up his heart to the battle of joy and of sorrow.

Homer, sovereign singer, was weaving the strands of his story,
Weaving together the threads of his life as he sat in his garden,
Where, on the path of the sea to the East, the island of Chios
Up from the waters throbs to the rise and the fall of the billows,
Being itself but a petrified fragment of sea-born music,

Which was sung into stone with its notes at their
　　sweetest vibration.
Over the slant and the summit the fruitage is hav-
　　ing a frolic,
Oranges coated with gold and olives sparkling in
　　silver,
Playing in floods of the sun that pour from the
　　sky to the island,
Whose new ardent blood is flowing to juice of the
　　wine-press.
Heart-beats of stormiest stone you can feel every-
　　where to the hill-tops,
Heaving the vehement earth till it rises from
　　slope into summit,
While the fiery soil is transmuted to grapes in
　　the vineyard,
Which reveal the red rage of the God in the
　　sparks of their droplets.
Pulses of passionate air you can breathe every-
　　where in the island,
Lifting the rapturous soul into love of the youth
　　and the maiden,
Which breaks forth into strains in answer to
　　valley and mountain.
Every look is a chorus of sea and of earth and
　　of heaven,
All of the isle is a song as it sways in the sweep
　　of its ridges,
And keeps time to the up and the down of the
　　beat of a master,

Tuning the sea and the land to vast undulations
    of music,
Notes of the strain that rose from the voice of
    the singer primeval
When he created the land and the sea and the
    firmament starry.

  In the heart of this musical isle, his birth-place,
    sat Homer,
And around him stood youths from the east and
    the west of all Hellas,
In a trance of the Muses carried along by his
    numbers,
Yielding their souls unto his to be shaped to
    that harmony splendid.
Nor from that group of fair youths could Eros
    be rightfully absent,
Eros, the God of Love, had his shrine, as his
    wont is, in secret
There in the garden of Homer who, though shut
    in his eye-sight,
Could behold each deity present, however dis-
    guised.

  Suddenly all of the eyes of the youths were
    turned from the singer,
And to the tune of new measures were shooting
    poetic scintillas,
Rolling sidelong in fiery joy, yet trying to hide
    it,

Flinging millions of sparkles over the form of a
    maiden,
Very beautiful maiden, who entered the gate of
    the garden.
Out of her hiding she moved, emerging from
    leaves of her arbor,
Like a Goddess she came, who has sped from the
    heights of Olympus
Down to the longing earth, to appear the divine
    unto mortals.
Forward she stepped to the group without stop-
    ping, and came to its center;
All of the youths were lighting her path with
    their looks as she passed them,
Making the twinkle of starlight there in the
    blaze of the sunlight.
With a reverent glance she touched the lean hand
    of the poet,
Yet the look of resolve gave strength to her
    face in its sweetness,
Softly obedience shone just while her own way
    she was going.
Standing behind him she pressed the bloom of
    her cheek to his forehead,
Roses of life seemed to suddenly shoot from the
    furrows of wisdom,
And to her father thus spake Praxilla the daugh-
    ter of Homer,
While her strong sweet lips gave a kiss which
    sounded heroic:

" Father, suffer me also to come to thy knees
 and to listen;
I would learn who thou art before thou pass from
 this sunshine,
Soon thou must go, methinks, with the Days, the
 daughters of Phœbus,
Go with the beautiful Days far over the sea to
 the sundown.
I am the daughter of Homer, hardly I know yet
 my father;
Do not deny me the hope of my soul which of
 thine is begotten.
Great is my longing to hear of what thou art
 saying and singing;
Why should men not share with the women their
 lore and their wisdom?
None the less will you have, and we shall gain
 much by your bounty;
We shall be worthy of you, and you will receive
 the full blessing.
Long I have patiently kept in my bower, my
 beautiful bower,
Covered with blossom and branch and filled with
 the fragrance of Nature,
Which thou nobly gavest me once — it seems long
 ago now —
Thoughtful the gift was and kind, but to-day I
 can stay there no longer.
As I listened within it, hidden in leaves and in
 branches,

Wreathed around and around in its flowers and
  clasped in its tendrils,
I resolved to go forth and to claim my heritage
  also,
Heritage equal of legend and song which are all
  thy possessions.
Hear me, O Father! thy child, I am come to
  know of thy knowledge,
I am come to thy school to learn if I be the true
  heiress,
And to say the one word which long has been
  growing within me,
Not yet mature, but this day it is ripe and must
  drop from my lips now:
Child of thy body I am, I seek to be child of thy
  spirit,
I, not knowing my father, am not the true
  daughter of Homer."

Mild was the mien, yet strong was the word
  which the maiden had uttered,
Gentle the note of her voice, suppressing softly
  a quiver,
Yet betraying a wavering line in response to her
  heart-beats,
Which sank down with her modesty, yet swelled
  up with her purpose,
Heedful of men in her presence, but of their
  scoffing defiant,

To her father dutiful, yet her own way she must
    go too.

　　All of the youths admired and looked, she re-
    turned not their glances,
Was there not one whom she in her heart already
    had chosen —
One of those beautiful youths, the flower of
    Hellas and Asia?
See how handsome they stand in a group, as if
    they were God-born,
Gathered now on Olympus, rejoicing their par-
    ents immortal!
Still not a look from the maiden that way! not
    a glance of sly favor!
How can she help it? But not a beam hath she
    dropped there among them.
Say, has Nature lost her authority over the
    maiden?
Once revenges were wreaked on the rebel, double
    revenges,
Love which rejects will feel too the pang of being
    rejected,
Twofold the wound which Eros inflicts if you tear
    out his arrow.
Mark how the generous summers of Chios have
    given their bounty,
Given their hidden command in the warmth of a
    Southern climate,
But the command is not heard, is defied by the
    daughter of Homer.

Subtle and sinuous are the retreats in the heart
    of a maiden
Where she hides herself, unconsciously testing
    the gold there;
Labyrinth hopeless it is to dozens of fairest of
    suitors,
Yet its clew is simple — merely the love of the
    right one,
When he happens along, as he certainly will, on
    her pathway;
Yes, he will come, though we cannot tell when —
    to-day or to-morrow;
Thinking or thoughtless, guilty or guileless, lo!
    he is chosen,
And the rest, much better perchance, march off
    under judgment;
Just he, nobody else, and the reason without
    any reason,
Sent from above he must be, it is said, yet sent
    by himself too,
Helped divinely she is, in going the way that she
    pleases,
Providence brings them together, and both have
    done what they wanted.
See the two Gods, within and without! they have
    met and are kissing,
Eros and Psyche have met and are kissing, the
    spirits immortal,
Long before the two mortals have tasted the lips
    of each other.

But not so it runs now in the tale of the
    daughter of Homer,
Now the law seems changed — and yet we can
    hardly believe it;
Strange desire she has to share in the lore and
    the legend,
Firmly refusing to listen to-day to the whisper
    of Eros,
Who is wont to be hinting to maidens his secret
    suggestion,
And to speak with his face hid in clouds till he
    dare be discovered.
Now she will take her part of the gifts from her
    father descended,
Dimly dreaming perchance that she hereafter
    may need them;
She will learn the old songs which treasure the
    wisdom of peoples,
Learn the story of heroes tried in the failure
    and triumph,
Learn the story of women, unfallen, fallen, for-
    given,
Faithful Penelope, dire Clytemnestra, beautiful
    Helen;
She too will sing, remaining forever the daughter
    of Homer.

    Gently the poet groped for her hand, reaching
        out with his fingers,

Found it and laid it in his with a satisfied look,
  then addressed her:
" Daughter methinks thy voice has suddenly
  changed from thy childhood,
Yesterday thou wert a girl, to-day thou art wholly
  the woman,
I can hear in thy tones once more the voice of
  my mother,
Thine is the voice of Cretheis, when she was tell-
  ing a story,
Sweet are the turns of thy tongue in talking our
  living Hellenic,
And yet seeming to speak just to me from a world
  resurrected,
Building anew out of speech the rainbows of
  youthful remembrance.
But a difference, too, I can hear — thy words
  are the stronger,
Yes, far stronger are thine than the words of
  Cretheis my mother,
Who could fable the past and loved antiquity's
  custom ;
Stronger I deem them than Helen's, which held
  in their spell all Achæa.
They do not dwell in old days, nor do they de-
  lay in the present,
They belong not here in our Chios, belong not
  in Hellas,
But reach out to a time and a land somewhere in
  the distance,

Dreamily rising this moment, I see, out the fog
  of the future,
Faintly lifted to life in the light of the beams of
  Apollo,
Who has whirled in his chariot over the arch of
  our heavens,
And, now facing the West, is scanning the far-
  thermost Ocean.
List! I bid thee to come when done is the duty
  of household,
Come when thou wilt and stay when thou canst,
  both now and hereafter,
Freely unfold what is in thee to all that ever
  thou canst be.
Travel thou must thine own way of life as thy
  father before thee,
Be thou child of my spirit, be thou heiress of
  Homer,
Follow the path of the Sun round the world, and
  that be thy journey."

Scarce had he uttered the word, when stately
  he rose from the settle,
Full of the thought he had spoken he shone in
  each line of his visage;
Then he moved to the place where stood in his
  garden an altar,
For, though blind, he knew well the way to the
  shrine of the Light-God.

After him moved the daughter and youths in
    holy procession,
Solemn, slow-stepping, while stainlessly white
    fell the folds of their garments;
When they had gathered about him and stood in
    a worshipful silence,
Hopeful he turned to the sky, rolled upward his
    sightless eyeballs,
Seeking the face of the God that shone as the
    sun in the heavens,
And he prayed his soul's prayer, with might of
    an instant fulfillment:
"O Apollo, bearer of all that is good to us
    mortals,
Bearer of light to the Earth and of sight to the
    soul in thy presence,
God of the luminous look that darts to the past
    and the future,
And doth shine on the present forever, creating
    it daily!
Shed still over the Earth thy light, though to me
    thou deny it;
Build thy arch of pure beams each day round the
    heavens above us,
Spend thy blessing on others, though I be not
    able to take it;
Hold overhead as our lamp and our shield thy
    canopy golden,
And, as thou risest upon the beautiful world out-
    side me,

Rise and illumine the world, the dim world that
 is lying within me!
Deity though thou be, for thee also I lift up my
 prayer;
Thou unfold in thyself while I too in thee am
 unfolding,
More and more may thy light be transformed
 from the outer to inner,
Till thou be risen from godship of nature to god-
 ship of spirit.
Then through thee may the song that I sing be
 reborn in the ages,
Ever reborn unto men in the sheen of thy spirit,
 O Light-God!"

 All the youths prayed the prayer of Homer,
  the daughter prayed with them,
In low tones of devotion that speak to the deity
 present,
Standing full in the sheen of the sun by the shrine
 of Apollo,
Who from his way in the West, threw back his
 glances propitious,
Warming the words of the poet, and making the
 moments all golden.

IV.

Erato.

The Stranger of Northland.

ARGUMENT.

At this point a stranger appears in the school of Homer, not a Greek or Asiatic, but a Barbarian, so called, from the far northwest. He has come to learn something about Homer, having had some previous information from a Greek captive whom he had taken in war. The stranger wishes to carry Homer's poetry — the whole of it, and not some fragments — to his people, and hand it down to the future. Meantime Praxilla, the daughter of Homer, listens to the story of the stranger with an interest never felt before, and she neglects for a moment her household duties in her eagerness to see and hear him. Homer and the scholars, after trying in vain to pronounce the rough gutturals of his name, salute him by the Greek title of Hesperion.

Scarce to the God of the Light had they ended
their powerful prayer,
And looked up from their service divine with a
sense of their freedom,
Lo, a stranger arrives, a youth still dusted with
travel,
Yet with a glow of new gladness that told of a
journey completed.
" Look, who is that?" the scholars were whispering each to the other,
" Homerid novel he is, just come from Barbary
distant ;
Wonder if he have a tongue in his mouth that
can trill the Greek accent,
See but his mantle of motley and garments
swaddled around him,

Look at his face and his form, he never was
    born in our Hellas.
Beautiful still he might be, if he only were
    dressed in our drapery."

Then they ceased, for the stranger already was
    standing among them,
Manly in look and lofty in stature and earnest in
    feature.
Fair was his hair and ruddy his cheek and broad
    were his shoulders,
Swift was the flash of his eye, it was wild and
    still it was gentle,
Often it sank to a dream reflecting the blue of
    the heavens.
Some new sort of a man he appeared to the
    Greek of the islands,
Taller he stood by the half of his head than any
    one present;
At the entrance he stopped and gazed at the
    group for a moment,
Smit by the sight of what he had suddenly seen
    in an eye-shot;
Then he turned and spoke to the poet, slowly
    pronouncing
Each Greek word in a tone that tingled the ear
    with new music,
Though it tickled at first the light-brained youths
    to a titter,
Whispering, jibing, making remarks in the ban-
    ter of boyhood.

Thus spake the stranger, deliberate, yet intoning his firmness,
For a message he had in his heart, and was going to tell it:
"Far in the region of snow I dwell, whence Boreas chilling
Falls on the sun-loved South with his sword that is forged in the Northland,
Forged out of ice and tempered in blasts from the nostrils of frost-gods.
Fierce is that warrior of winds and like the barbarian ever,
Who is charmed from his frozen world to the warmth and the harvest,
And descends to your seas with his hordes in a whirl and a tempest,
Mad with your love he smites in his rage and seizes your beauty.
But, Oh Homer, you I address, the goal of my travels —
For I deem you that man whom I name by the awe of your forehead —
Do you know your measures have pierced our ice builded fortress,
Warming our clime by their breath and melting our hearts to their music?
Rude is the turn of your words in our speech, and dim is the meaning,
Still it touches our hearts, and to sympathy softens our fierceness;

You have made us all feel ourselves a little more
 human,
When your Hero in wrath relented in pity for
 Priam,
Ransomed his bitterest foe and comforted sweetly
 the father.
Northland is starting to thaw in the breath of
 the Southern singer,
And I am come to reward you alive by telling
 the message."

Joyful the poet was tuned by the tidings hyper-
 boréan,
Voice from a far off world and promise of much
 that was coming,
Casting across the Greek landscape a shadow of
 lands in the sunset.
New were the tones of the tongue, not Doric,
 Aeolic, Ionic,
Not the turn of the speech that is spoken on
 island or mainland,
Nothing like it had ever been heard in the city of
 Chios,
Nothing like it had ever been sung in the strains
 of a rhapsode,
Music it had of its own, and yet all the words
 were Hellenic,
Nay, all the words were Homer's, and seemed to
 be drawn from his poems,

Wondrously tinged with new tints and quaintly
  turned to new meanings.
Greatly surprised at the sound of the voice spake
  Homer, uprising:
"Speak, oh guest, tell how you have learned
  our language of Hellas;
Hard it is for the native, harder it must be for
  strangers,
Cunning it is like ourselves, eluding the grasp of
  the learner,
In its hundreds of shifts transforming itself like
  old Proteus.
Then I notice your rhythm to be of my measures
  begotten,
And some turns of your speech are certainly born
  of my spirit,
Aye and the sweep of the thought when you
  spoke of the Hero Achilles.
Well you have heard my song, far better than
  many a Grecian,
Though a barbarian, you, I can feel, have the
  touch of my kinship.
Mighty and marvelous is all this, I would never
  have thought it,
Come now, tell me the story, Oh guest, for great
  is my wonder."

"That I shall tell you at once," he replied,
  " not long is the story.

What I have spoken to you, I learned from a
    Greek, my own captive,
Whom I had taken in war, when he came to my
    country's border,
Trading, plundering, wandering over the world
    for adventure;
That was another Ulysses, much-enduring and
    crafty,
Loving the song and the fable, singing them too
    on occasion,
Loving the deed and daringly doing on land and
    on water.
Your Greek earth was too small for the stress of
    his thought and his action,
Over the border he broke and hunted his prey
    like a lion,
Knowledge beyond it he sought, and fell into fate
    in his searching.
How I felt in my bosom the swell and the stroke
    of his spirit!
When I found what he was, I made him my friend
    and companion,
Though a slave still in name, he was given my
    love and my bounty;
Well he repaid the act; from a prisoner's death
    I had saved him,
And he saved me in turn from the ignorant death
    of the savage.
There in the forest your speech I began, I prac-
    ticed it daily

Till by his aid I was able to speak it the way you now hear me.
Him I set free as soon as he taught me the language of Homer,
It is the word of your poem that broke the chain of his bondage,
Mine too it broke at a blow when I said in your Greek: 'Be free now,'
And I am sure, it would break every chain of the people who spoke it."

More astonished than ever the poet burst out into questions:
"Why hast thou come to this spot, and how didst thou get to our island?
Utter again to me here thy broken Hellenic — I love it,
Love it twisted and splintered and broken to radiant fragments
Dropping out of thy mouth, yet speaking the best that is spoken.
Say, who art thou, man, and what art thou doing in Hellas?"

Jubilant Homer asked, but could not wait for the answer,
Asked once more, and that was not yet the end of his asking,
Till the stranger, breaking the lull of a moment, responded:

" He the Greek whom I spoke of, once called
    you a native of Chios;
With that name in my heart, inquiring each step
    I am come now
Over the land from afar and over the sea in a
    vessel.
But is it so? I can hardly believe it myself —
    Art thou Homer?
Tell me, old man, thy name, O speak it but
    once — Is it Homer?"
  " So I was called by my mother, still so I am
    called by the Hellenes,
Though there be some who deem me not Homer
    but some other person,
Merely a different man of that name," responded
    Homerus,
And a sunrise of smiles broke over the seams of
    his features,
As arose in his thought the pedagogue dwelling
    in Chios,
Terrible pedagogue, trouncer of boys, the crusty
    Typtódes.

   Then spake the stranger, uplifting himself to
       the height of his stature,
Far overlooking the heads of the rest of the little
       assembly:
" Let me now tell you the scope of my travel,
       the hope of my journey!

Praised be the Gods! I have reached in safety
the place of your dwelling,
Mighty, resistless the need I have felt to see you
and hear you,
Aye, to learn your full song and store it away in
my bosom,
Whence the Muses, daughters of Memory, al-
ways can fetch it.
I would carry it off to my home far up in the
Northland,
Fleeting over the wintery border of beautiful
Hellas
Where it reaches beyond the abode of the Gods
on Olympus,
To the regions where drinking their whey dwell
the mare-milking Thracians,
Over the hills and the valleys away to the banks
of a river,
To the stream that is bearing the flood of the
wide-whirling Istros,
Still beyond and beyond, still over the plain and
the mountain,
Over vast lands to the seas, and over the seas to
the lands still,
Through the icicled forest, and through the
tracts of the frost-fields,
Still beyond and beyond, still over the earth and
its circles,
I would carry your song in my soul to the homes
of my people

Where the huge arms of the breakers are smiting the shore of the Ocean,
Ever beyond and beyond in the stretch of their strokes they are striking,
Beating, forever repeating the strokes of the infinite Ocean."

Both of his arms he outstretched and gazed on the sea for a moment;
Catching his breath, the stranger returned from his look to his hearers:
" Barbarous lands and peoples you call them, and truly so call them,
But in their hearts they are ready, I know, to be tuned to your music,
And to be dipped, once more new-born, in your harmony holy,
Which they will keep forever enshrined in their lore and their legend.
Homer, O Homer, poet of all the nations and ages,
Give unto Barbary now what the Gods have given to Hellas."

Round whirled the stranger, the beat of his thought still smiting within him,
Driven out of himself, he walked at a whisk a small circle
And came back to his stand, as if putting a bodily period

There to the sweep of his utterance swift, but
　　his spirit's full gallop·
He could not rein in at once, and so his words he
　　continued :
" All of your song I would know, the whole
　　of it fitted together,
That Greek captive of mine could only sing me
　　the fragments,
Broken off here and there from the whole —
　　most beautiful fragments,
Which Mnemosyne fleetingly brought him when
　　he invoked her.
But the whole of your song I must have, the
　　whole of it shredless,
For the whole is often far more than all of its
　　pieces,
Aye, the whole is all of its pieces, and is the
　　whole too."

Here laughed Homer aloud, yet spake no word
　　with his pleasure ;
What had started the poet who rarely gave way
　　to his laughter?
It was the thought, the comical thought of the
　　pedagogue Chian,
Who was always beating and breaking the song
　　into pieces,
Till he became what he made, became too himself
　　but a fragment —

Terrible fragment of man, the trouncer of boys
　　and of verses,
Terrible pedagogue Chian, the slasher and
　　thrasher, Typtodes.

All of the youths drew closer around him, the
　　wonderful stranger,
Scholar hyperboréan, the first that had come from
　　the Northland;
They received him as one of themselves in the
　　school of the master,
Gone is the scoff and the jibe, and the whisper is
　　speaking respectful.

Also Praxilla was there, the beautiful daughter
　　of Homer,
Hearing the marvelous tale and pondering deeply
　　its meaning.
Sweetly the maiden looked up and smiled at the
　　mirth of her father,
Though she knew not the cause, she knew that
　　the stranger had pleased him,
Her too the stranger had pleased, she thought,
　　in pleasing the father,
Her too the stranger had pleased — she knew not
　　what was the reason.
Not yet brought to an end was the task of the
　　day in the household,
Still she lingered and listened, though hearing the
　　call of the kitchen.

Nobly erect stands the youth, and towers aloft
    in his stature,
Brave as a hero he must be to travel alone the
    long journey,
Loyal the heart in his breast, so true to his Greek
    benefactor;
Lofty his soul looks out and full of divine aspi-
    ration!
Man with a beard, overtopping the cluster of
    beardless bardlings,
As great Zeus overtops all the Gods in his mien
    and his power.
Burst is the bloom of his manhood, still as a man
    he is youthful,
Weighty his speech drops down with the ring of
    the masterful doer;
And Praxilla the daughter of Homer still lingered
    and listened,
Lingered to hear but a word, one more word
    she would catch from the stranger,
Though again she heard the importunate cry of
    the kitchen.

Seeing her there he began once more, that son
    of the Northland,
For he thought she might wish to be told what he
    knew about women:
"Rude though we be and warriors from birth, we
    are fond of the household,

And we honor the wife who rules with her heart
    in her home life;
But, yet more, we honor the woman, for she is
    the healer,
Ever the merciful healer through the love in her
    nature,
Healing the soul and the body, and nursing the
    sick and the helpless.
Aye, yet more, we hold her the seeress, the
    gifted divinely,
Who has the vision beyond, foretelling the time
    unto mortals."

And Praxilla still lingered and listened, the
    daughter of Homer,
Lingered to hear but a word, one more word she
    would hear from the stranger;
Louder and louder resounded the dolorous cry
    of the kitchen.

Then the poet in speech forethoughtful and
    hearty addressed him:
"Welcome, oh stranger, here is our board with
    its wine and its viands,
Stay and partake, be refreshed from thy journey
    in body and spirit,
First pour a drop to the God of the Light, far
    darter Apollo,
Pray then, for men have need of the God, he will
    answer thy prayer.

Take of me all that I am, or was or ever I shall
 be,
Bear me afar as thou wilt, to thy folk in the
 snows of the Northland,
Learn all my song and carry it off, the whole,
 not a fragment,
For no fragment can live if torn from its life in
 the body;
Sing it thyself and let it be sung by the farther-
 most peoples,
Thine it is as it is mine, if thou only art able to
 sing it;
In thy words I can feel that thou art the son of
 the future,
Feel what is coming to me and to mine from the
 world to the westward.
Welcome O guest, now drink of our wine and
 eat of our viands;
Stay — perchance I shall make thee joint heir of
 all my possessions."

So spake the father in joy, expecting the feast
 to be ready.
But Praxilla, where is Praxilla, the dutiful
 maiden?
Still she lingered in spite of herself, and listened,
 and wondered,
Lingered to catch but a word, one more word,
 from the lips of the stranger,

Though her father she heard re-echo the cry of
kitchen,
When he spoke of drinking the wine and eating
the viands.
Beautiful daughter of Homer she stood there,
but dutiful also;
She was restless, and said to herself in reproof,
still delaying:
"Surely I ought to be off, I was needed long
since in my kitchen;
What will the household become if left to itself
in the future?
Oh, those women, those wonderful women, up
there in the Northland!
That was the tale of a dream, and still I appear
to be dreaming,
Thinking myself far away in the glistening home
of the frost-gods,
Thinking myself in a temple of ice on the top of
an iceberg.
Woman, now speed from this old Greek world
and march to the new one!
Would he take me along if I perchance would go
with him?
That is my mind — and yet I know not whether I
know it;
That is my mind — beyond the seas and over the
mountains —
But I must go — my kitchen, my kitchen — and
still I delay here —

Ever beyond and beyond is my mind, on the wings
  of my thinking,
Over the plain and the mountain, and over the
  border of Hellas,
Up to the stream that is bearing the flood of the
  wide-whirling Istros,
Over the river afar to the shore of the further-
  most Ocean,
Where I can feel the embrace of the waves of the
  earth-holding Ocean,
There I would stand by the waters — and yet
  even they could not stop me!
But away to my kitchen, my kitchen — Oh, why
  do I stay here!"

Just at that moment the stranger looked over
  the youths round about him,
But those youths did not mark quite what he was
  warily seeking,
Even away from the poet he looked and found
  what he searched for,
Where stood the lingering, listening daughter of
  Homer, Praxilla,
Who still delayed for a word, one more word
  from the lips of the stranger.

  Then spake the father, breaking into the
    thought of the daughter:
  "Hold! thy name, O guest, we must know, ere
    we go to the banquet,

We must address thee as one of our own, when
    we sit at the table."
  Slowly the stranger pronounced it, barbarous,
    heavy, rough-throated,
But those soft-toned Greeks could not speak it in
    spite of their cunning,
Oft he repeated it for them, but in vain they
    essayed it,
Rudely its sounds were jolting out their mouths
    in confusion,
Broken to fragments around on the air flew the
    name of the stranger.
Then the master spake out, and bade all be silent
    a moment:
  " Much too old is my voice to be forced to the
    tones of thy language,
Always it creaks and breaks if strained to the
    subtle adjustment,
I have sung too much to make any longer this
    discord.
Hearken to me! in my tongue I shall name thee
    henceforward Hesperion,
Son of the Evening, come from the dip of bright
    Helius westward,
Rising and shining when it is sunset already in
    Hellas.
That is a name we can sing to right music in
    measure Hellenic,

List to the word, let us sing it together: Welcome, Hesperion!"
Then the youths sang aloud all together: Welcome, Hesperion!
And Praxilla whispered in silence: Thrice welcome Hesperion!
In a blush at her whisper, she turned and ran out to her kitchen.

Clio.

The Travels of Homer.

ARGUMENT.

Homer takes up the account of his travels through Hellas in preparation for his work. All his scholars are present, of whom a short list is given. He first went to Troy, and saw the ruined city with its plain, where the war took place. Then he crossed over to the continent of Greece, and heard the people of each village celebrate the deeds of its special hero. While singing himself he also heard the bards of every locality sing its special legend of Troy and the aforetime. Thus Homer gathered all the stories of the Trojan war, and fused them together into his great national poem. He chances to speak of Helen and her captivity; at once the old conflict flames out among the pupils in his school. But Homer stops the dispute for a short time, and continues the narrative of his travels, till the strife breaks out anew, this time over Hector, between Glaucus the Lycian and Demodocus the Ithacan. Each side is still ready to fight the Trojan war over again. Homer once more harmonizes the conflict, and takes occasion to show how the poet must embrace in himself both sides of the struggle which he portrays.

Morning had come from the East saluting the
island of Chios,
Throwing her kisses of light along every line of
the landscape,
Till it stood forth in her glance, revealed and
transfigured to vision.
Soft was the light that she dropped from her lips
on the hill and the valley,
Tenderly touching the air with violet tinges and
golden ;
Under her feet lay the waters and over her head
bent the heavens,
Both of them waked from the night, reflecting
her soul in their stillness ;
Sea and sky, the two big blue eyes of nature, had
opened,

And were looking with joy on Chios, the beautiful island,
Where not far from the beach stood the garden and dwelling of Homer.

All the youths had assembled to hear the tale of his travel,
Which by the chance of the moment had been before interrupted;
Now they would hear of the way he had wandered to come to his poems,
For they all would like to be Homers and sing of the heroes,
Catching the glory of life in the lilt of a musical measure.

Glaucus was there, a youth from the banks of the eddying Xanthus,
Mighty his ancestor was, Bellerophon, hero of Lycia;
Warriors his race had been, but he now sought to be poet;
Singing not doing the deed he held the better vocation.
Other great names were present from lowland and upland of Asia:
Gyges, Mysius, Nastes, son of a Phrygian monarch,
Dardan from Gargarus nigh unto Troy, the city in ruins,

Aphroditorus the curled Milesian boy, Niobides
Fresh from the tears of Sipylus — these may
    stand as examples;
But the foremost was Glaucus, the son and the
    grandson of Glaucus,
Far back tracing his blood to the veins of Bel-
    lerophontes.

Next, O Muse, thou must glance at the youths
    who crossed out of Europe.
Young Demodocus came, who sprang from an
    order of singers,
Living in Ithaca where they sang of the toils of
    Ulysses.
Homer had been their guest when he touched
    their isle in his travels,
Gathering wonderful Ithacan tales of voyages
    westward,
Fabulous threads of song, like gossamers floating
    in sunshine,
All to be caught by the poet and wove to a beau-
    tiful garment.
Teucer of Salamis came, descended from Teucer
    the archer;
Skill in handling the bow he possessed — the
    gift of Apollo,
But the God had refused his other great gift —
    that of wisdom;
Still the youth would be singer, and broke in
    scorn all his arrows,

Talent he had for the one, desire he felt for the
 other,
Teucer could not what he would, and whatever
 he could he would not.
Burly Plexippus was there, the richest scholar
 of Homer,
Glossy and sleek were grazing his herds in
 Thessaly grassy,
Thousands of horses were his that drank at the
 streams of Peneios,
Palaces too he owned and held whole cities for
 barter;
Somehow he thought he could simply exchange
 some cattle for verses,
E'en the Pierian spring was his by virtue of
 money,
Once for its waters he counted out pieces of gold
 and of silver,
But though their fountain he bought, he never
 could purchase the Muses.
When he returned to his country and held his
 Thessalian domains,
All his thought was to buy up the home of the
 Gods, high Olympus,
Then the Gods he deemed he possessed, possessing
 their mountain,
And at his will he could call them down from their
 heights to his poem.

 Other youths from the islands had come, and
 also from Argos,

But the Muse has not given their names excepting
 Sophrones,
Clear Athenian soul, devoted to worship of
 Pallas,
Moralist ever was he, the manifold maker of
 maxims.

Tall Hesperion too was present, just from the
 Northland,
Sole barbarian there, yet eager to learn and to
 listen,
Towering over the rest like Fate over beautiful
 Hellas;
Strong were his features, yet melting to love in
 the sunshine of Chios.

One more scholar forget not, though first present this morning!
There she stands behind by the door — the daughter of Homer,
Still by the door in the rear — she yet will advance to the foreground.
Shy are her glances, striving to hide her heart in
 her bosom,
But they are tell-tales, and whisper the thought
 she is secretly thinking.

Voices arose which bade the poet go on with
 his story;
Grappling awhile for his thought again he began
 his recital:

" First I went over to Troy, and dwelt on its
    plain and its hillock,
In the city destroyed I stayed and lived with its
    ruins,
Which still talk to the traveler telling their story
    so fateful.
Rivers I saw in the plain, and heard the God of
    Scamander
Speak of the Heroes slain and many a furious
    battle,
As he pointed to corselet and helmet and shield
    mid his rushes,
Showing the skulls of the dead that grinned from
    the ooze of his stream bed.
Thence I passed on the sea in a ship from island
    to island,
Felt the favor of hoary Poseidon, and felt too his
    anger,
When he would roll up the waves in a storm by
    the might of his trident;
Him I once saw in his chariot scudding away on
    the billow
Right into sunset, and leaving a fiery track
    through the waters.
Glad for my life I was when I came to the main-
    land of Hellas,
Peoples I saw, their cities and customs, but
    chiefly their legends
Drew me to listen and gather each radiant shred
    of their spirit.

Heroes unknown I found everywhere, great men
 of their village,
Whose high deeds were at festivals sung by their
 townsmen in worship,
For each village its Hero must have and revere
 him divinely.
Every bard in the country I heard and stored up
 his fables,
Till the Delphian cleft which utters the measures
 prophetic,
Till the Thesprotian land where speak the oaks of
 Dodona,
Till the Olympian heights where Gods look
 down upon Hellas.
And to Helicon came I and heard the song of its
 Muses,
Singing a rival strain to the Sisters who sit on
 Parnassus;
There I listened to Hesiod, crabbed old singer of
 Ascra,
And I gave him a note of the song that was rising
 within me,
I had already begun the new lay of the Gods and
 the Heroes.
For a moment he ceased his complaints of man
 and of woman,
Quit his dark world of monsters primeval and
 hazy huge Titans,
Just long enough for a laugh to break out like a
 flash from a storm-cloud,

And to say to me: Friend, I shall visit thee
  sometime in Chios."

Here the poet himself was a smile and dropped
  into silence
For a minute or more, and then he returned to
  his story:
"Early to Argos I came and heard in a hymn the
  whole people
Chanting the glory of Diomed, who was their
  valorous leader,
How in the war of Troy he fought with the
  Gods, though a mortal,
Fought with two Trojan Gods in the might of
  his heart, and he conquered;
For the Greek though a man, must put down the
  God if a Trojan.
'That' I said to myself 'is a note in the lay of
  our Hellas,
In the grand lay of our Hellas that is a strain of
  the music;
Part of the one vast temple of song in the soul
  of the nation,
I shall take it and mould it and build it into my
  poem.'
Each little fragment of life and each stray film
  of a story,
Name of mountain, river and town, whatever I
  found there,

All I picked up on the spot, and began to weave
 them together,
By the aid of Mnemosyne, Muse who always re-
 members.
 Then to Mycenæ I went, the golden, where
  dwelt Agamemnon,
Through the portal I passed that was guarded
 above by the Lions,
Fiercely glaring in stone at the man who entered
 their gateway.
Much the splendid city had waned from its old
 Trojan glory,
And the look of the sunset rested all day on its
 towers.
There I learned the King's fate at the hands of
 his wife Clytemnestra,
And the death of herself and her lover, both
 slain by Orestes.
Sad was the tale of the doomful House of the
 Monarch wide-ruling,
I could never refrain from repeating that tale in
 my measures,
Truest example, methinks, of the dealing of
 Gods with us mortals,
Still to be sung in many new poems to millions
 hereafter.
It will be poured into bronze, and hewn out of
 whitest of marble,
Told in tongues yet unborn, to measures unheard
 of in Hellas.

Wretched indeed is the man, if the Gods in his
    pride, he obey not;
Base Ægisthus, I feel in my heart the point of
    thy dagger!"

  Fervidly spake the old man, and he seemed
    overcome by his story,
Thinking the fate that befel the great prince
    of the Greeks, Agamemnon.
To his own life the poet transmuted the lives
    of the Heroes,
Every thread of a fable he span to a strand of
    his heart-strings,
Each wild word of the wildest old legend he
    caught and transfigured,
Unto each sorrow of mortal his bosom beat
    mighty responses;
Nobly the youths were led to revere the man in
    the poet.

  Soon his gloom he had caught and flung it far
    back into Lethe,
Whence at times it escapes in the brightest of
    souls up to daylight,
And he began, in his countenance looking the
    look of the sunrise:
" Over the heights I scrambled, that was a coun-
    try of mountains!
Woodmen I met in the forest, here and there a
    small hamlet,

But every where I could find some fragment of
 song or of story.
Through the glens I passed of the piping Arcadian
 shepherds,
Through the hills full of music down into the
 vale of Eurotas,
Where lay Sparta — and there was the home of
 the beautiful Helen.
Still the palace I saw in the sunlight, where Paris
 the Trojan
As a guest was grandly received by the King
 Menelaus,
And I saw too the glance of the eye and the
 thought of the woman,
In its first flash to the fateful resolve — of wars
 the beginning!
Madly I followed each step on the path of the
 sea as she fled thence,
Feeling the glow and the guilt of a passionate
 world in each heart-beat,
Watched her enter the ship, the sheltering ship of
 her lover,
Watched it ride on the sea till it vanished afar on
 the waters.
There I sank on the sand, as the dead man drops
 from the arrow
Sent to his heart, and I died for a while in the
 battle of Helen.
O Aphrodite, Goddess of joy that is paid with
 all sorrow,

Queen of the love that bears in its proof the bitterest vengeance,
There I fell down the thrall of thy spell, but I rose up the master.
Thou dost also possess in thy right the soul of the singer,
I was Paris myself and I fled to the East with my Helen,
Troy I was too and its siege, I was taken and burnt into ashes;
But I am also the law which is read in the flames of the city,
And I am the stern judgment of Gods who speak from its ruins."

When the poet had stopped in the rush of his words for a moment,
See! a youth stands forth with a flash in his eye like a falchion,
Lycian Glaucus it is, from the banks of the eddying Xanthus,
Grandson of Glaucus who fell in the war by the walls of the Trojans,
Sprung of the seed of Heroes, though poesy now he has chosen;
Standing forth from the ranks of his friends, thus says he to Homer:
"Helen belonged to our side, for she was the woman of beauty,

We had to take her and keep her, or lose the
　　heritage lovely,
Basely resign it to others, and yield up the claim
　　of fair Asia.
Twenty years she was ours, of all the great war
　　she was worthy,
Twenty years she was ours, and we paid but the
　　price of a city,
Even one moment of Helen is worth all the losses
　　of Priam."

Scarce had he done when a valorous youth
　　sprang out of the front-line
From the opposite ranks, as if to respond to the
　　challenge;
It was Demodocus, son of Demodocus, Ithaca's
　　singer,
Now in the school of the poet to learn the new
　　song of the ages;
Far in advance was the song of all that were sung
　　in his country
By the old bards, his fathers. Pointing his finger
　　at Glaucus,
Raising his arm and smiting the air at each word,
　　he spoke thus:
" Yes, we smote you, we burnt you, we bound you
　　when sated with slaughter,
Women we seized and your wealth, we wasted
　　the city and country.

Little was left in the land, in your gore we
    painted our glory,
And the same fate awaits you again if you come
    to the trial.
Helen, the prize of the world, you had to sur-
    render forever."

  Each of the fiery speakers had spoken his speech
    in a fury;
See the turn! how strange! they are looking no
    more at each other.
Both of them bending the head, they covertly
    glance at one object,
Right at one point where stands the beautiful
    daughter of Homer,
As if Helen she were, to be fought for and won
    by a nation.
But in the background quite overtopping them
    all stood the stranger,
Just behind the fair daughter he stood and
    seemed to be weighing,
Dreamful, blue-eyed Hesperion, yesterday come
    from the Northland,
Now he seemed to be weighing two weights in
    the scales of a balance.

  In the midst of the din the poet uprose from
    his settle,
As great Zeus on Olympus, the God of the Greeks
    and the Trojans,

Who looks down to the earth and judges the
    struggle of mortals.
Homer suddenly saw the old conflict arise in his
    scholars,
Every battle at Troy was still in them — how
    could they help it?
From the East and the West they had come, from
    Hellas and Asia,
Deep is that scission of soul and of time — a
    breach everlasting,
Not to be healed but by one who is both the
    victor and vanquished,
Who can feel the defeat triumphant, the triumph
    defeated,
Who can be slayer and slain, and rise up new-
    born from his ashes.
Homer united both sides, and both saluted him
    poet,
What in them was a discord, he turned into har-
    mony lasting,
What was twain in their lives, in his he made one
    and a poem.
All had their own completeness in him, so hailed
    him as master.

When to speak he began, one word changed
    strife into concord:
" Hold, O youths," he cried, " cease wrangling
    at once in my presence;

Learn from to-day just what is the bondage you
 are to get rid of:
Free is the poet, but free you are not when ruled
 by a passion;
Whole he must be, but whole you are not when
 halved into parties;
Music you never will make if the soul hath a
 break in its tension.
Hear entirely; now let us go on with the rest of
 my story.
Over to Pylos I passed, and saw the land of sage
 Nestor,
Who returned to his home from the war un-
 troubled by tempest,
Or by the wrath of the Gods, which wrecked so
 many returning.
Older than I am he was when at Troy, and yet a
 good soldier,
Fond of the fight, but of telling a tale of his youth
 still fonder.
Thence I sailed to Ithaca where I heard of
 Ulysses,
Wisest of men, he endured; and enduring, he
 rose in his wisdom;
Great were his deeds at Troy, for he was the
 Hero who took it,
Mounting its walls by the wooden horse that was
 winged with his cunning;
Over Achilles he rises, through might of the
 spirit's contrivance.

But yet greater his task was after the city had
    fallen;
To return was the Hero's work, to return to his
    country
And to his wife, through storms of the sea and
    himself in his doubting.
Wandering through the whole world that lies out
    the sunlight of Hellas,
Into the magical islands beyond the bounds of
    our knowledge,
Suffering sailed he on, though losing all his
    companions;
Ithacan bards there told me his tale of the Cyclops,
    of Circe,
Even through Hades he passed, through the realm
    of spirits departed;
Living, the Hero must go beyond life, and return
    to the living.
Thither I followed him too, in my age I told his
    adventures,
Bringing him back to Penelope prudent and
    Ithaca sunny;
Last of my song is this, it has just lately been
    finished,
Though some parts have been sung long since at
    the festivals Chian,
Showing a glimpse of the West where men find
    always their new-world."

Thus he spake, and he turned, though blind, with his face to the sundown,
Where in his path Hesperion, thoughtful, was standing in silence;
But before he began, interposed Sophrones of Athens:
"Why such a liar and rogue did you make him, your hero Ulysses?"
"Penalty too he must pay, the penalty even of wisdom,"
Answered Homerus, thoughtful, forecasting his words for his scholars.
Low and slow he now spoke, as if with his soul he were talking:

"Always the deed must be paid for, the doer heroic must suffer,
Virtue arouses revenges and duty may call up the Furies;
Double the conflict must be, and the right may also be double.
O Ulysses, great was thy action, but followed by curses!
The reward of thy life will be centuries full of reproaches!
Wrongful men thou didst pay with their wrong, for this expect judgment;
Thou didst meet the guileful with guile, smite foes with their weapons,

Thou shalt be rated as guileful and cruel in turn
  for thine action.
Compensation, the law, has been laid by the
  Gods upon me too,
All the sunshine of nature is dark in spite of my
  vision,
Insight the Muses have given, but for it my sight
  has been taken."

Such was the answer, but it met not the need
  of Sophrones,
Who was the moralist trying old tales with the
  touchstone of virtue,
Easily solving the problem heroic by rule or a
  maxim,
Excellent maxim for men who have not the stress
  of the problem.
Thus the worthy Sophrones tested the life of the
  Hero,
Putting his standard to each and measuring
  strictly the defect.
Hear him again, for always Sophrones has one
  other question:
" Which was right, the Greek or the Trojan?
  That is the point now,
Truly the point to be settled before I can enter
  this calling.
Much I have been worried about it, and still no
  decision.

Ere I can sing, I must know just what is and
    who are the righteous.
Dare I confess? I like not Achilles, Ulysses,
    not Helen,
Beautiful Helen — she is not beautiful seen by
    my vision,
Nor can I love Penelope prudent with all of her
    cunning;
Aye, the Gods of Olympus I like not, I cannot
    adore them;
Zeus do you think I can worship, a God with the
    passions that I have?"

Homer, the poet, was silent; Sophrones, how-
    ever, grew louder:
"Best of them all is Hector the Trojan, the man
    most perfect,
True to the wife of his heart and doing his duty
    to country,
Brave as a lion in war and gentle at home as a
    woman.
But, like the good man always, he had to fall in
    the struggle,
And by fate to lose what he fought for — his
    cause and his city.
Such is the world — the great men are bad and
    the good men must perish."

On the spot the sparkles were flying from one
    of the scholars,

It was Glaucus who spoke, the fiery Lycian bard-
ling:
" He was right — great Hector — defending
his home and his nation
From the wanton attack of the bandits who sought
to destroy them;
Valiant in every way he was for his land and his
people,
He is the Hero of Homer, I say, the only true
Hero;
Hector was right, will be right forever, and he was
a Trojan."
Then he turned to one of the company seeking
approval,
Just from one and no more he sought it — the
daughter of Homer,
Not from the father the poet, but from the beau-
tiful daughter
Sought he the meed of a glance for his verses,
but she beheld not,
For she was looking away from the youths in an-
other direction.

But in answer Demodocus spoke, his vigorous
rival,
Rival not only in verse, but also in love of the
maiden:
" Yes, but he fought for the thing that was
wrong and he knew it — your Hector!

For the rape of Helen he fought and made it his
  own thus;
Aye, the good husband battled in Troy to keep
  wife from husband.
What in his soul he condemned, he supported by
  arms and by words too,
And so died of a lie in his life and the spear of
  Achilles."

Suiting the act to the speech, Demodocus drew
  back and lifted
Hand and arm to a poise, as if he were hurling the
  weapon
Straight at Hector, to slay him before the battle-
  ments Trojan;
Lycian Glaucus shrank not, but leaped to the
  front at the challenge.
Great was the uproar; the war of Troy once
  more was beginning
Right in the school of Homer, but quickly the
  master bade silence:
"Hearken, O youths, what I say, and learn
  by example a lesson!
Not a part is the poet, nor is he owned by a
  party.
On which side do I sing in my poem — the Greek
  or the Trojan?
Mark it — on both and on neither; the will of
  Zeus is accomplished,

God supreme of the Hellenes, rising above all
  conflict.
Not with another, but with himself is the poet's
  true struggle,
He is the slayer and slain and his soul is the
  place of the battle.
Much I think with the Greeks and much I feel
  with the Trojans,
These have my heart perchance, but those take
  hold of my reason;
Zeus too loves his dear children in Troy, but de-
  cides for Achæa.
Ah, the poet must fight in himself the dolorous
  combat,
As the God fought the God in the fray on the
  heights of Olympus;
Wounds he cannot escape, he must bleed in the
  battle on both sides;
Showing the strife of the time, he shows too the
  strife in his bosom,
But he must heal it — just that is the seal of the
  God on the singer;
Rage, war, battles he sings, but also the peace
  and atonement,
Sings great Achilles in wrath, and reconciled
  sings great Achilles.
Now let the truce be confirmed between both
  the Greeks and the Trojans,
And in our joy we shall pour to the Gods a hearty
  libation."

Tall Hesperion silently heard the dispute of the
    bardlings,
Much he had learned about Hellas, and seen the
    two sides of the conflict,
Seen it still living and parting atwain the new
    generation,
Who were ready to fight over Troy, and over its
    poem.
But the best was, he saw the poet bring both
    sides to oneness,
Out of discordance bring harmony lofty of men
    and of Gods too,
Making the tumult of war sing the song of
    Olympian order.

Homer in happiest mood uprose and continued
    his talking:
" Youths, Demodocus, Glaucus, now heal ye the
    wounds of each other,
Thinking the thought of high Zeus, as it sings to
    a melody god-born,
Speaking divinity's word which is sprung of the
    soul's recognition.
Valiant ye be, but let us proclaim, the war is
    now over,
All in one joy to-day let the East and the West
    greet as brothers,
Each of them taking the best of the other as
    test of his spirit!"

Turning aside, he spoke out the word of command in a transport: .
"Speed thee, Amyntas, my boy, a full jar of old Chian, the oldest,
Ten years' ripe let it be, for age in the wine bringeth wisdom
Back to the drinker, in concord attuning anew the lost temper,
Bringing the oneness of truth into souls that differ by nature.
Here comes the wine, already I catch a whiff of its fragrance,
Oldest of Chian it is, a God would mistake it for nectar.
Glaucus, Demodocus, Gyges, Plexippus, and Aphroditorus,
Noble Hesperion also, thou valorous youth of the Northland,
Pledge now a health to yourselves, and pour to the Gods a libation."

All the youths of the school, most willing, obeyed the good master,
Touched loving lips to the brim of the wine on the rim of the beaker,
Pledging a health to themselves and pouring to Gods a libation.

Hark! mid the draught a shrill noise is disturbing the flow of the liquid,

'Tis the rickety gate as grinding it grates on its hinges.
Opening first to a push, then backward it slams with a racket;
What is the shape that noisily enters and shuffles along there?
Man well-known in Chios he is, well-known unto Homer,
Satisfied man with himself he seems by the turn of his features.
That is the pedagogue, first of the island, the lord of the laurel,
Which he doth use as a switch for teaching the verses of poets,
Teaching the boys of his school the glory and gift of the Muses,
Whose fair branch he now twirls in his hand as he turns up the pathway.
Terrible pedagogue Chian he comes, the thrasher and slasher,
Thrashing the youths into lore and slashing the poets to pieces,
Into the school of Homer he walks — he is here — O Typtodes!

VI.

Terpsichore.

The Pedagogue Chian.

ARGUMENT.

A rival school to that of Homer is taught by Typtodes, the Chian schoolmaster, who comes one day to have a short visit with the poet. Typtodes is the severe critic of Homer's poems, and cuts them to pieces quite as some modern professors have done. But the schoolmaster is a progressive man and is now specially interested in the new script which has been brought from Phœnicia. In fact he is giving to the poems of Homer their first alphabetic dress in spite of his criticism. It turns out that Typtodes has really come to see the daughter of the poet, though he disguises the fact. But his bitter criticism is modified by the wine which Homer causes to be brought him, and his final questions are in a different vein from his first utterances. A new man appears who will give some answer to what Typtodes has asked.

Not alone and unchallenged the poet held sway
   in his city,
There was a rival in Chios, who in his realm was
   the ruler.
Most of the youths of the place were sent to the
   school of Typtodes,
Crusty Typtodes, a far-famed trouncer of boys
   into learning,
Tickling bare legs of Greek boys till they danced
   to the sprig of his laurel,
Which he always held in his hand while he made
   them con verses,
Rousing the Muses unwilling by use of their
   favorite symbol.

Some were verses struck at a heat from the heart
   of a poet,
With an Olympian might, and flowing and glow-
   ing forever
In the fire and flash of the words of the primal
   conception.
But the others, the most, were his own, the pedagogue's verses,
Made without a mistake according to rule in his
   school-room,
Flawlessly made out of wood, the toughest wood
   in the forest.

In his sandals he shuffles along the loose stones
   of the pathway;
Slyly he shuffles and seems to be slipping about
   on his tiptoes,
As the schoolmaster warily slippeth around in
   the school-room,
Seeking to catch in the act the bad boy who is
   making the mischief.
Gaunt and ungainly the man, and somewhat
   stilted in posture,
Sparse was the beard, each hair from his visage
   shot out like a bristle
Ready to stick and to prick any person approaching too near him,
Even the kiss of Typtodes had the keen point of
   a briar.

Thin was the nap on his garment, exact each step
 that he took there,
Always the branch of the laurel he held in his
 hand while walking
Had in its swaying upward and downward the
 look of precision.
Sharp was the thrust of his eye, as it peered from
 the hole of the eyebrows,
Slightly barbed was the point of his nose, no
 mercy allowing,
No escape for the foe; his whole visage seemed
 pointed and ready,
Even his look was a cut and his tongue had two
 edges of sharpness.
Yet the man had his virtues — industry, feeling
 of duty,
Faith in knowledge he never gave up, in spite of
 reverses,
And, on the whole, he believed in the movement
 of men to the better.
Bearer of light to Chios he was, when the day
 was beginning,
Homer he was not, and yet but for him there had
 been no Homer,
Whom he first put into script from the word and
 made everlasting,
By the skill which he had in tracing Phœnician
 letters.
 This fair day he has come to have a good visit
 with Homer,

Whom as a man he liked, as a fellow-craftsman
    respected,
Deeming himself to be, however, the much bet-
    ter poet,
Though the world had passed on the men a differ-
    ent judgment.

   He had heard of the beauty, too, of the daughter
       of Homer;
Living in the same town all his life he never had
    seen her,
Never had seen her, though knowing by heart
    every word of her parent.
Not too young to be curious, not too old was
    Typtodes,
Pedagogue Chian who sought for a glimpse of
    the beautiful maiden,
Though, of course, he pretended to come for a
    chat with the father.

   Settled down in his seat he began to talk of his
       methods,
How the rule had been found, and the glory was
    great of the finder.
" Yes, methinks I have brought to perfection this
    science of teaching !
Surely not much will the schoolmaster have to be
    doing hereafter
But to follow, ages on ages, the steps of Typtodes.

What great progress to-day we are making in
    every department! ·
Some weeks ago a new churn was invented by
    Phagon of Samos,
Hither he brought it at once and showed it around
    in our island;
Soon each household of Chios will have it, soon
    will be churning,
Churning away for dear life the milk of the kine
    of the country;
Barbarous oil-eating Greeks will change into
    eaters of butter,
That is improvement, that, I call, the grand
    march of the species!
Only one fear I cannot help feeling amid all our
    progress;
All the world will have nothing to do, and so will
    do nothing,
After that we are gone, and have left it the fruit
    of our labor;
Idleness is the great curse, our children will have
    to be idle;
Such is my fear; so I one day have resolved to
    take easy;
Having dismissed my school, I would dally awhile
    in your garden,
Leave the words of the poem behind and talk with
    the poet."

 Here he stopped for a moment and slyly was
    peeping around him,

Once, twice, thrice he looked, and every look was
 a question,
Asking, "Where, I wonder?" but without any
 answer,
Though he could hear a sweet stray note now and
 then from an arbor.
In its stead unwilling he heard the voice of old
 Homer:
"Friend, have you any new light on the dark way
 of life? — O give it —
Some fresh word upon fate or the law or the
 wonderful secret;
Eyesight is gone, and often I feel the bounds of
 my insight;
Often I feel the bounds of the word in the stress
 of the spirit."

Then began in the height of his mood the pedagogue Chian:
"We have lately been reading, or rather reciting
 your poems,
Since in the school or the market they still for
 the ear are recited,
Though I myself can read those recent Phœnician
 symbols,
Catching the sound of the voice in the devious
 tracery of letters;
I alone of all of the men in the island of Chios,
I can wind out the labyrinth weird made of
 strange Alpha-Beta,

Follow the clew to the end and bring back the
    prize that is hidden,
Hidden away by a spell in the heart of the char-
    acters mystic.
Into those signs I have been transforming the
    voice of your verses,
Scratching the musical sound into signs which
    now are called letters,
Magical symbols of fast-fleeting speech, which
    fix it forever,
Holding it firm to the sight when the tongue
    which spake it, is silent.
But not yet I have seen your beautiful daughter,
    Homerus,
Whom Fame whispers abroad in every nook of
    our Hellas."

" O good man," said the poet, " aught more
    would I hear of this wonder,
Which has caught and is holding the word to
    make it eternal ;
Fate forbids me to see it, Oh then let me learn of
    the marvel
Changing the world at a stroke by giving the past
    to the future."

Crabbed Typtodes perchance was not pleased
    with the turn of the answer,
But he began on the spot to speak out the thing
    that was in him:

" Let that pass — all that which I said of Phœnician letters.
We have glanced these days down into the depths
of your poems;
Now I am going to speak you the word of friend-
ship and frankness.
You, I find, are not accurate, shifting the dates
of your action,
Not quite correct in the facts, and you give your
twist to the story.
All your tales of the Gods are turned to the
bent of your thinking,
Somehow changed from the old they seem to be
bearing your impress.
Often you make in your spring important mis-
takes in the measure,
Short where it ought to be long, and long where
it ought to be shortened,
Forcing the stress of the voice in places where it
belongs not.
And I hold the hexameter is not fit for your
poem,
Which, so rapid in movement, should not be
delayed by the meter;
If you only had asked me, I could have told you
a better.
Nay, I deem that measure not suitable to the
Greek language,
Which has a boisterous genius not to be swaddled
in long clothes;

You should remember from Troy the Greeks no
  longer are babies.
Hark to a verse of your poem, describing far-
  darting Apollo,
Which should be simple and rapid and grand,
  divine in its movement;
Slowly it drags along and cumbers its flight with
  its lumber,
Then at the end it suddenly whisks and swashes
  its tail round.
What a blasphemy! Phœbus will take from his
  quiver an arrow,
Sly invisible arrow, penalty due to the Muses,
Put the notch to the bow-string and pull it — behold! who is stricken!"

Warmed to his work was shrilly Typtodes,
  and so he continued,
Cruelly lashing himself into slashing to fragments the poet:
"And that mixture of words from every part of
  our Hellas,
Mixture poetic of fragments of speech from
  island and mainland,
Doric, Ionic, Æolic, how can it ever be lasting?
It is a wonder that people to-day are willing to
  hear it;
No such jargon has ever been spoken by Greek
  or Barbarian,

Crumbs from the table of tongues — and that is
    the language of Homer.
Though to nature it be not kin, still I put it in
    writing,
And I study it too, though I have to tear it to
    fragments;
What seems substance turns in my hands to the
    flimsiest shadow,
I confess I have pleasure in knocking nothing to
    pieces,
All to pieces I knock it so that it appears to be
    something."

Satisfied well with his work, Typtodes contin-
    ued in judgment:
" Nor are your characters always consistent,
    however heroic,
Diomed changes, Ulysses is never the same in
    two stories,
And your implacable Hero is placated twice in
    his anger.
Homer himself is never the same, but shifts to
    another,
Dozens and dozens of Homers I find ensconced
    in your verses.
Your large poem doth fall of itself into many
    small poems,
Which, I know, were sung by hundreds of singers
    before you,

Who were the primitive makers of what you have
  gathered and taken;
You are but a collection of songs, a string of
  loose ballads,
You are not one and a plan, but many you are
  and planless.
Now I shall state to your face the final result of
  my wisdom:
Homer, aye Homer himself is not the true author
  of Homer."

Up rose the pedagogue Chian and stretched to
  the height of his stature,
Whirled his ponderous arm as if a boy he were
  flogging,
Slashing the verses of Homer, a pupil he seemed
  to be thrashing,
Terrible pedagogue Chian, the slasher and
  thrasher Typtodes.

But in response he called up the cheerful humor
  of Homer:
"Take my book and study it further; perchance
  you can read it
In that new sort of script which you say has come
  from Phœnicia.
One is the book if you are one and can ever be
  happy,
Wholeness first being found in yourself, is found
  then outside you,

I am halved and quartered if you are a half or a
    quarter,
But a whole I shall be, if you are a whole in my
    study;
Discord enough you will find in my poem, if you
    be discordant,
Discord enough in the world if harmony to you
    be wanting.
But those wonderful letters — would I might see
    them and read them!
Ere I pass from this earth, I would know the
    Phœnician letters!"

Mild was the manner and sweet was the voice
    of the godlike singer,
Dropping transparent as pearls the beautiful
    words of his wisdom,
Showing in chilly old age the upspring of young
    aspiration.
But that terrible fragment of man, the trouncer
    Typtodes,
Spake once more, and showed in his voice a dash
    of resentment:
" My next business will be to cut up your book
    into ballads,
I shall put the keen knife of this brain to each
    joint of your body,
Though I be but a half or a quarter, or less than
    a quarter,

You shall be smaller than I am, you I shall chop
  into mince-meat."
" In dissecting, oft the dissector himself is
  dissected;
What to another he fits, may fit just the fitter,"
  said Homer.
" What a prophet you are? In you I foresee the
  grand army
Who will cut me and stab me with every sort of
  a weapon,
Gashing and slashing my whole poetical body
  to fragments.
Still I affirm your army so grand can never defeat
  me,
I shall remain as I am, the wounds will return to
  the giver.
But let us stop this pitiful wrangle, it wholly
  untunes me;
Harmony, wisdom, hope it hath not, but ends in
  mere nothing.
Cheerful now let us pour to the Gods a hearty
  libation,
Then let us pour to ourselves a good draught in
  the warmth of our worship."

Mellowed at once to the rhythm of wine Typtodes gave answer:
" Now you are truly a poet, with fresh inspira-
  tion you touch me;

Wine is a poem in drops, which you easily sip in
 small verselets;
That hexameter which you just made while urging libation,
Was a good one — the best, to my taste, you
 ever have spoken.
Better, I think, I shall now understand the drift
 of your verses."

 Look! a beautiful figure has flitted past to the
 garden;
Is it a sudden dream, a phantom of vision fan-
 tastic?
No; Typtodes has caught a glimpse of the
 daughter of Homer,
Caught one fitful glimpse of the shape of the
 beautiful maiden,
More he longed for and looked for, but he received not the second.

"Now I would know," he said, "how you build
 with such skill your grand temple,
How you turn your soul into music that flows in
 your measures,
How you turn all the world into harmony wedded
 to beauty,
How you call down the Gods themselves from the
 heights of Olympus?"
"Bravely," the poet replied, " you aim at the
 white of the mark now;

But it is not my calling to point out the path of
the Muses
In their flight through the air down to men from
the top of Parnassus.
Surely enough it is if I hear them when they are
singing,
And repeat their melodious strain in its fullness
to mortals.
Faint is the note at first, but it goes on extending
and swelling,
Till it sweeps to its musical train the whole earth
and the heaven,
Tuning the discord below and above, of men and
of Gods too."
" But whence cometh the world of the Gods and
their sway on Olympus?
To the beginning I wish to return and make my
inquiry."

So spake Typtodes, when a new figure rose
over a hillock
Walking out of the distance, amid the orchard of
olives.
" Aye, whence cometh the man, who goes to the
Houses of Hades?
What is he here for — the mortal of clay once
shaped by Prometheus?
And the woman, his mate, the beautiful, fateful,
what is she?"

Asking he glanced to the right and the left for
  the daughter of Homer,
Nowhere he saw her, but in her stead he beheld
  through the leaflets,
Slowly approaching, the man he had seen before
  in the distance.

Such were the questions which eager Typtodes
  put to Homerus,
Who replied not, but seemed of something else to
  be thinking.
Hark to the groan of the gate which suddenly
  grinds on its hinges!

VII.

Melpomene.

The Singer of Ascra.

ARGUMENT.

The person approaching turns out to be Hesiod, the poet of Ascra in Bœotia, whom Homer had met in his travels and whom he had invited to come on a visit to Chios. Hesiod is received by his brother poet, and tells his story of the Gods, and his view of the world. He, too, will see and know the daughter of Homer, though he has no good opinion of woman. Finally he beholds her, when, for a sarcasm on her sex, she gives him a tart reply. The old Greek misogymist and pessimist slips away from the company, and vanishes out of Chios at the appearance of another woman, the songstress of Lesbos.

All start up at the stridulous sound to see what is coming,
When a stranger moves into the path of the eye to the heavens,
Leisurely comes down the walk which leads to the garden of Homer,
Beautiful garden of fruit and of flowers, of shade and of sunshine.
Broad and bony the hand of the man, and knotted the knuckles,
Trained to whirling the ax by the helve in the woods on the mountain,
Trained to holding the plow by the handle in turning the furrow,
Used to toil were his palms, and hardened to horn by his labor.

Great strong lines he had in his face dividing it
 crosswise,
Also dividing it lengthwise to network of valley and mountain,
Which would rise and fall into billows of rough
 corrugations:
Surely that face was a battle, the battle of Gods
 and of Titans,
Seizing and hurling volcanoes aflame in their
 wrath at each other.
Under his features was lying a scowl, which
 seemed to be born there,
Which would dart from its lair in his look, spit-
 ting fire like a dragon;
Strange was the tone of his speech, yet stranger
 his play of grimaces,
Lips would writhe at each word, as if it were
 sore to be spoken.
Hark! he is ready to speak and turns to the poet
 of Chios:

 "Over the sea I have come in a ship from the
  mainland of Hellas;
 Voyage unblest, for Poseidon was trying each
  minute to drown me,
 Dashing his waves on the craft and mightily
  cleaving the waters;
 Often he opened his jaws and shut them tight on
  the vessel,

How I escaped I know not, but salted and scared
  I escaped him.
Heavy Bœotia is my home, my village is Ascra,
Ugly village of Ascra, vile in the summer and
  winter.
There I sang of the Birth of the Gods and the
  Works of poor mortals,
Mortals, who sweating and swinking in life, die
  at last in a discord."

" What a note is that in the sunlight of Chios,"
  cried Homer,
" Who art thou, man? Some tricks of thy voice
  I have heard in my travels."
Twisting his face into scowls, as if he were tasting
  of wormwood,
Spake the poet of Ascra, and spitefully spat out
  the bitter:
" Well thou knowest, for thou hast borrowed
  some of my verses,
Hiding the source in a word, thou hast called it
  the breath of the Muses.
Once I sang for thee when thou hadst come to
  my home in thy journey,
Sang of the eldest Gods who were born of Chaos
  primeval,
For I like to go back to the start, though it be
  all in darkness,
Origin ever I seek, although I can never quite
  reach it.

What a pleasure to run from the sheen of the
    sun back to nothing!
This Olympian order of thine, it came of dis-
    order,
Which is my burden of song reaching back to
    the very beginning;
Even this beautiful day now sporting in joy of
    the sunshine,
Not long ago was born of the night and to night
    it returneth."

"Hail, O brother," said Homer, the bard, to
    the poet of Ascra,
"I have heard thee before on Helicon — now I
    remember —
Bleak was the day and hoarse was the wind that
    blew up the valley.
Be at home, O guest; give us more of thy song —
    I would listen."

Then again the poet of Ascra seemed tasting of
    wormwood,
Ere his strain he began in the stress of a mighty
    upheaval;
Soon into thunderous words he let out the soul
    of old Chaos:
"All this isle, this world, as we see it, was once
    but a monster,
Peopled with monsters grim in the grey of the
    distant aforetime;

There I love to dwell with old Cronus who swallowed his offspring,
Even to Uranus oft I go back for a gaze in the twilight,
And I dally with Nereus, parent of beautiful daughters,
Thousandfold forms of the billows'rising, rolling, retreating,
Fleeting forever away in the haze of the distant horizon,
Leaping anew into life as they rise to the top of the sea-swell.
O for the mightiest monsters of old! I tell you, I like them;
All day long I could sing of the terrible brood of the Gorgons,
Triple-headed, hundred-handed, thousand-legged,
Cerberus, Briareus, Hydra, Chimæra, Echidna the lizard;
What is Olympus to these, with its Gods who dwell in the sunshine!
Once in this world lived a people I loved — the Giants and Titans,
Who could hurl as weapons of war huge mountains and rivers,
Heaven itself they would storm and break down the limit of mortals,
Which the Gods once set in their envy when man they created.

Long the battle was fought, the stormers of
 heaven were vanquished,
Now see them whirl — down, down they spin to
 Tartarus sooty,
By the Olympians whisked off the earth-ball to
 infinite spaces,
Where they lie under ban of falling, falling for-
 ever.
Still in the Upperworld sunny they wrought for
 the ages great wonders;
This fair island, this sea, yon mountains are
 showing their power.
Lofty, grandiloquent words are my colors, by
 which I can paint them,
Words that are sung in mine ear by the high
 Heliconian Muses,
Loving the mighty and monstrous and piling up
 horror on horror"

"Hold, for mercy!" cried Homer, "let me
 catch breath for a moment,
For I seem to be falling, falling along with your
 Titans,
Down to black Tartarus whirling I spin in a
 spiral headforemost.
Poet, is there no light in your world, no beauti-
 ful order?"

Curling his lip to a scowl, responded the singer
 of Ascra:

"I cannot say that I like your Olympian sunshine, Homerus,
All of your deities stand too clear in the sweep of my eyesight,
Cut into words they walk as if they were moving to marble,
Gods in my thought should break over bounds into limitless regions,
Break over all of the forms of fair life into infinite fancy.
Give me the view far away o'er the deeps of Oceanus hoary,
And his thousands of children with all the dim train of the sea-gods,
Breaking, creating their shapes with every new dash of the wavelet,
Riding the steeds of the sea and leaping from billow to billow.
Homer, I come to pay thee a visit once promised at Ascra;
And I have heard of a beautiful maiden now dwelling in Chios."
"Welcome again, O friend," said Homer: "some wine in a goblet,
Speed thee Amyntas, my boy — some Chian wine for the poet."

But the musical guest in response made a face full of discord,
For in spite of himself he longed to behold the fair daughter.

Disappointed, he turned once more to the tale of
    his terrors:
"Dragons I love, if human, and forms of the
    sphinxes and griffons,
Forms commingled of man and of beast, which
    sprang from the Orient.
You, O Homer, have driven my monsters away
    to the background,
Far in the background of Hellas they lie under
    curse of your spirit,
Where they will stay by your spell, I fear, in
    the darkness forever.
— No, again they will rise," spake the poet of
    Ascra prophetic,
"Out of the night they will rise and bask in the
    sheen of Apollo,
Far in the future I see them step to the light
    from their hiding,
They will riot around in the world as in times of
    the Titans,
Storming Olympus again in the might of their
    struggle for heaven,
They will battle with Gods on the earth and the
    air and the ocean,
Till the Underworld sunless will rumble and
    quake in its terror."

  Here a youth stepped forth, he had recently
    come from the Northland,
Tall Hesperion, who from a dream had been
    roused by the story,

Roused by the mention of Giants, the dwellers of
 mountain and iceberg,
Calling to mind his own far country in landscape
 and legend.
Thus he spake in response to the poet of Ascra
 foretelling:
"Truth you have spoken, I know it; those mon-
 sters are living and thriving
Just at this moment far up in the nebulous tract
 of the Northland
Where they fight with the fire and sport with the
 frost of the icefield;
Mighty and massive those Giants of cold, the
 Hyperboréans,
Never I thought I would find them here in the
 sunbeams of Hellas,
Even in story I did not expect to be told of their
 wonders,
Though they be sitting in Tartarus sooty, the
 cheerless, the hopeless.
Tell me your name, O stranger, for I would
 carry it with me,
When I return to my land with the name and the
 song of great Homer,
Both of you banded together shall go to my home
 in the Northland."

With a gleam of rude joy responded the singer
 of Ascra,
Fame he reproached and despised and yet he
 longed to be famous:

"I am called Hesiod, younger in song than Homer, yet older,
Earliest Gods I have sung and the latest of all — Prometheus,
Friend of poor lost man, and the sufferer, too, for his goodness;
Sufferer God-born he lay in his anguish on Caucasus lonely.
But the strange spell of my life! I cannot get rid of the woman!
On me has rested a curse, the curse of that charmer Pandora,
Once created by Zeus, endowed by each God with his talent,
Born with craft in her heart, then sent upon man for his evil.
Off and away! good Homer, I whisper the hope of my journey!
Much I have heard in my land of a girl now grown to a woman,
Can I not see, perchance, now converse with the beautiful maiden?
Vain is my visit to-day if I see not the daughter of Homer;
More than Helen she is, aye more than the gifted Pandora."

"Here comes Amyntas," said Homer, "bearing the fragrance of Chios;
What a perfume of the wine as he steps in the gate of the garden!

Well, that boy is a flower that blooms with the
  scent of old Bacchus!
I can trace his path in the air without hearing his footstep.
Drink now a cupful of tears that were shed on the
  beautiful island,
Tears of the wine-god which tell not the sorrow
  but joy of the godhood."

Hesiod turned up the cup, and drank off the
  vintage of Chios,
Generous vintage of Chios, that lightens the soul
  of the singer.
And that cup was a wonder, with figures that
  danced in a circle,
Forms of maidens and youths that danced in a
  ring round the wine-cup,
Wrought by the cunning of Chalcon the smith, and
  given to Homer,
When in his youth he sang for the prize and won
  in the contest,
Won the fair prize in a contest with deep-toned
  Ariston his teacher.
So they sipped off the wine from their beakers a
  moment in silence,
Hesiod, Homer, the great Greek singers were sip-
  ping together
There in Chios the wine that is good for the Gods
  and us mortals,
Good for libations to Gods and a slaking of thirst
  unto mortals.

Soon they were done, for they loved, not the
    frenzy, but joy of the wine-god.

"Dearest my daughter, where art thou?
    Come hither and lead me," said Homer.
But he heard no response, so he called out again:
    Praxilla!
What is the matter? where is the maiden? Gone
    on an errand?
No, she was looking just then in a dream from
    a nook of her arbor,
Whence she could gaze on the fair-haired, blue-
    eyed youth of the Northland,
Wondering what she would do if she went to
    the folk of the icefields.
Of a sudden she woke from her wonder and
    sprang to her father,
Speaking mid blushes: "I was not gone, behold,
    I am present."
But the flashes of red spake louder that what
    she had spoken,
Truer than words in telling the truth of the heart
    that is hidden.

Then they passed from the house for a stroll
    mid the trees and the vineyard,
All together they went — the youths, the guests
    and the maiden.
Shady the roof overhead of the leaves and the
    twigs and the tendrils,

THE SINGER OF ASCRA.

Leaves of the olive with silvery sparkle in sunbeams of Chios,
Tendrils of grapevines that clasped the twigs in tender embraces,
Hinting of love in a bower to hearts that are young, and to old ones.

Hesiod saw with delight the beautiful daughter of Homer,
Every seam of his face was illumed with the torches of Eros,
Fled are the monsters aforetime, ended the battle of Titans,
And the wormwood of words is turning to sweetness of honey;
Glances he cast on the maiden and coined them to lines of a poet.
Singer of Ascra, thou hast forgotten thy tale of Pandora!

Also Typtodes beheld in a joy the daughter of Homer,
For the pedagogue too was a man, though dry in his learning,
Dry the vast heap of his learning, but it would make a great bonfire,
If but one little spark would snap from the flamelet of Eros,
Fall on the ponderous pile and suddenly set it to blazing.

O Typtodes, pedagogue Chian, what are these
    flashes!
Thou hast forgotten thy letters, forgotten the
    symbols Phœnician.

  So they walked and they talked till they came
    to the view of the waters,
Wondering came they at once to the side of the
    sea everlasting
Rolling its waves from beyond and beyond, far
    over the vision,
Over the tremulous line where heaven and earth
    run together,
Where the God may be seen as he comes and de-
    parts from the mortal.
Nearest the billow that broke on the beach stood
    the maiden Praxilla,
Just behind her with look o'er the sea stood
    youthful Hesperion.

  All of them gazed at the waves, and thought-
    fully dropped into silence,
Seeming to peep far over the bound of the bend-
    ing horizon
Into the realm beyond for a moment, and hear
    its low music,
Feeling a gentle attunement of soul to the beat
    of the billows,
Telling the pulse of the world that is coming, the
    world that is going.

List to a voice! a herald is hurrying out of the city,
Running along the white sand of the margin that gleamed in the sunshine;
"Hearken," he cried, "I announce the approach of the sovereign woman,
Poetess come from the Lesbian isle to pay homage to Homer."
"What! a woman poetic!" broke out old Hesiod crabbed,
With a twinge in his lips as if tasting his words that were wormwood,
With a whirl of his fist as if fighting the Gods like a Titan:
"What new evil is born to the suffering race of us mortals!
This last woman, methinks, is worse, far worse than the first one,
With the gift of her verses she comes, far worse than Pandora."

"Hater of woman!" quickly responded the daughter of Homer,
Why are your Muses women, your own Heliconian Muses?
Long I have known of you here, I have heard that tale of Pandora,
Shameless! you have in that tale besmirched the mother that bore you."

Off slipped the poet of Ascra through a lone
 path by the sea-shore,
Thinking to catch some vessel awaiting the breezes
 for Hellas,
Eager to quit the sunshine of Chios for heavy
 Bœotia,
Leaving the Gods of Olympus, to dwell once more
 with the Titans.
Surly he sauntered along by himself till he
 passed out of vision,
Hapless poet of Ascra, dismissed by the daughter of Homer.

Meanwhile the rest of the people went back
 from the sea to the garden,
Where they sat down on the stones which were
 seats for the guests in a circle,
Waiting to hear the first notes of the beautiful
 songstress of Lesbos,
And with a festival high and a hymn to receive
 her with honor.

VIII.

Thalia.

The Songstress of Lesbos.

ARGUMENT.

The person heralded is Sappho, a poetess of the island of Lesbos, and ancestress of the later more famous Sappho. She had caught from Homer the spirit of song in her youth, and now she comes to tell him her gratitude for what he had done. She thinks that Homer, through his story of Helen, had helped to save all women of Greece, herself included, from the fate of Helen. She crowns Homer with a garland for his other pictures of noble women, those found in the Odyssey. At this point the daughter of Homer steps forward and asks Sappho concerning a secret. Hesperion, who has listened to the songstress and has heard her songs before, comes forward and asks a similar question. The result is, the two lovers are brought together through Sappho, the poetess of love. But they are suddenly separated by the warning sound of a trumpet.

Who could it be that had come from the neighboring island of Lesbos,
Lovely island of love, and the home of the lyre of Hellas?
It was Sappho, beautiful Sappho, poetess tender,
Singing ancestress of many a Sappho still greater than she was,
Sister own of the Muses, the sister too of the Graces,
Breathing the heart of her sex into strains of the sweetest of music,
Bearing the beautiful name to be borne by her children hereafter,
Sappho, melodious Sappho, first name of the songstress of Hellas.

Many a Lesbian woman she gave of her
    musical dower,
Tunefully sharing the gift of her song to the soul
    'that might need it,
All of them singing of love with the joy, the
    triumph, the sorrow,
Tasting the magical drop which wings with a word
    the sweet senses —
Lesbian bees that lit on each beautiful flower
    of nature,
Busily culling in song the bitter-sweet honey of
    passion.

 Sappho already had sung for the prize in a
    contest with Homer,
Years agone that was, when she was the bloom
    of a morning,
But when he was a noonday turning and looking
    to sundown.
Both of them sang before judges — the prize was
    a new-made tripod,
Fashioned to life by Chalcon with dexterous
    strokes of the hammer,
That it seemed ready to step and to walk while
    standing forever.
High and mighty the judges taken from lords
    of the islands,
And from rulers of cities on mainland, all of
    them greybeards;
Rigid and just they were deemed in settling dis-
    putes of the people,

Rigid and just were the judges, and still she had
    won before singing.
See but the gleam of her eye, no furrow of frost
    can resist it!
Every heart she had won by her look, and away
    went the tripod;
She herself was the song that sang more sweetly
    than Homer,
Love and beauty were hers while singing of love
    and of beauty,
She was the prize herself, the prize of the Gods
    to the winner.
No true Greek could ever behold her, not hoping
    possession.
So the tripod she easily won from the first of
    the poets,
By the decree of the judges, whose law she took
    in her triumph,
Took too the hearts of the greybeards along,
    and they could not help it;
Homer himself in their place had not given
    another decision,
Homer had turned against Homer, had he been
    one of the judges.

But to-day she harbored no thought to tell of
    that triumph,
Rather ashamed she was, for she knew the power
    that gave it.

Years had brought to her life the golden return of their harvest,
Still not chilling the warmth and the glow of the Lesbian summer.
Not too young in her folly, not too old in her wisdom,
Almost repentant her spirit looked out on the world from its windows,
Casting its glances adown as if it had a confession.
Stately she moved, yet modest, into the presence of Homer;
Courteous welcome he gave to the songstress, when she began speaking,
Not in her own soft cadence, but tuned to the sweep of his measures:

"Thee, O fatherly singer, I come to visit in Chios,
Chios, thy beautiful island, fair sister it is to my Lesbos;
I would behold thee once more in the living form of thy features,
Ere thou pass to Elysian fields, last home of the poets,
Who shall dwell as spirits beyond in the house of their genius,
House of high fantasy built, material stronger than granite,

Holding eternal the echo of musical strains of the
singer.
There among thine own Heroes, there abiding
forever,
Thou the Hero shalt be thyself — in the deed the
first Hero;
For of all thy great people of song, thou singing art greatest,
Singing high actions of men thine action itself is
the highest.
There I too, a poet mid happy Elysian meadows,
Hope in the sound of thy song with thee to be
living immortal.
But to-day I have come once more in the sunshine to listen,
I would hear thee again this side of the pitiless
earth-stream,
And would speak thee a word — not to thee but
to me it is needful,
Bringing thy soul nearer mine — the word of
sweet recognition."

" Aye, it is sweet, that word," interrupted the
poet good-humored,
" Even to age it is sweet, for myself I do not
deny it;
More I would hear of thy strain, so deftly thou
turnest thy measures."

Seeing herself reflected in Homer, the songstress continued:

"Long ago I first heard thee attune the high lay in my Lesbos,
I was a girl in my home, and thou wert a wandering minstrel,
Who went singing through Hellas the wrath of the Hero Achilles,
Singing the fateful, dolorous tale of the beautiful woman,
Wandering, singing, and tuning thy song to the hearts of the Hellenes.
Helpful thou spakest to me in the bloom and the peril of girlhood,
Mighty thy voice in my heart just then in the struggle of woman;
At thy command my soul was set free and broke forth into measures,
Irresistible measures of longing in Lesbian music.
Secretly sang I my earliest notes to a circle of maidens,
Who would listen and love along with the tender vibrations,
Singing the strains of the song and touching the strings of the cithern.
That was after I heard thee hymning the story of Helen,
How she was blinded and sank in the spell of sweet Aphrodite,
Though the Goddess she fought and rated with heavy reproaches;

How by Paris of Troy she then was led from her
    husband,
Going, unwilling to go, and yielding though
    always refusing,
Driving the Trojan away, yet drawing him back
    by denial,
No was the word of her tongue, but Yes the
    response of her action."

Here she stopped for a moment and looked
    abashed at her daring,
Thought unspoken when born into speech has in
    it a demon,
Who oft leaps from the sound of the word and
    frightens the speaker,
Till the courage returns to speak out the heart
    of the matter.
Poetess was the Lesbian, having the right to her
    color,
Having the duty to utter the truth of herself in
    her singing;
Warm were the tones and strong were the tints
    of the thoughts that she painted;
Though her words seemed growing forbidden,
    courageous began she:
"Must I confess it? Helen I felt in myself at
    that moment!
All of the bliss and the blight of her love swept
    over my heart strings,

Touching them lightly at first, then smiting them
    harder and harder,
As if I were a lyre by fingers of Fates to be
    played on,
Thrilling to music the ebb and the flow of the
    ocean within me,
Making the billowy passion sing to a measure
    responsive!
Willing unwilling, fated yet free, to myself but
    a battle!
Yes, I confess, the Goddess I felt, the Goddess
    resistless,
Driving me forward to do as did the beautiful
    woman,
Whispering dulcet commands in words of divin-
    ity's power.
Yet Aphrodite but spoke to what was within me
    already,
Willing, unwilling, fated yet free — ye Gods, how
    she smote me!
Till through the cleft of my heart I could see
    down, down to its bottom!
With the prize of the fairest, the penalty too has
    been given,
With the beautiful women is chained the spite of
    a Fury,
Who doth secretly lurk in the gift of the Gods to
    the mortal.
But I stand not alone, for all I now stand in thy
    presence:

Every wife in Lesbos, in Chios, in all the Greek
    islands,
And on mainland too, through Hellas, through
    midland of Argos,
Far in the isles of the West and over the sea to
    the sundown,
Has that danger of Helen, the lapse of the soul
    in its loving,
With the vengeance that follows the joy and the
    glory of beauty.
In thy story a witness I was of all that I might
    be,
Saw the dread ghost of myself and fled from the
    horrible specter!
Homer, my father, thou hast saved me from be-
    ing a Helen,
In thy song thou hast suffered and saved all men
    and all women
Winning thy soul to themselves in its story of
    trial and rescue.
I had been taken to Troy, if thy word had never
    been spoken,
All the daughters of Greece thou hast rescued
    from fleeing with Paris,
Though his city has fallen, again he had come to
    Achæa,
Were it not that thy song keeps the warning alive
    and the judgment.
Troy still stands in the world and holds in its
    citadel Helen,

Only in song, thy song, is it taken forever, O
    Homer."

There she stopped on the height of her thought,
    the Lesbian songstress,
Whence she could see far over the sky-bound
    limit of Hellas;
Soon in sweet low tones responded the poet
    prophetic:
"Gracious words thou hast spoken and dear to
    me, beautiful woman;
Singing the peril of beauty in soft, warm words
    of thy measures;
Muse among Muses the tenth for thy strain henceforth I shall name thee,
Aye, for thy love the tenth Muse I shall name
    thee to nations hereafter,
Who thy honor will sing beyond the far streams
    of the Ocean,
First of the women of Hellas to build the melodious poem,
Chastely chanting thy lay to the wives and maidens of Lesbos.
Thou wilt be followed by thousands of songsters
    along down the ages,
Thine is the musical prelude of forests of nightingales singing.
Women preserve the story and song as they
    nourish their infants,

Who must be reared on the voice as well as the
milk of the mother;
Nature makes her sing, she must die or sing to
her baby;
Motherly harmony is her first gift to her child,
and the greatest.
What a world I see rising before me, the world
of the woman !
Beautiful Helen again shall be sung, aye, more,
she shall sing too,
Taking herself Troy town, not conquered but
conquering Paris;
She shall be the new Hero Achilles, in action
heroic,
Gods! as I see I must speak! she also shall be
the new Homer."

Down fell the word like a blow, surprising
even the speaker,
Who by the spur prophetic was driven beyond
his own knowledge;
But on the spot she snatched up the talk, that
Lesbian songstress,
For she still had a weight on her heart to be
lifted by speaking:
"How we look at ourselves in thy tale of the
beautiful woman!
Our warm heart thou hast felt, its ready response
and the peril.

All our circle is drawn, the trial, the fall and the
    sorrow,
Then the return of the soul, the rise and the
    grand restoration;
Helen estranged is restored to her own, restored
    to herself too.
In her marvelous tale I can see the past and the
    future,
All the life of our people unfold to the story
    of Hellas.
But still more than Hellas I watch in the lines of
    her image: —
This whole round of existence on earth, hard
    destiny human,
With the rise and the drop in the struggle of good
    and of evil,
Now on the up and now on the down of the life-
    stroke eternal,
Measuring cycles of pain and of gain to the beat
    of the master."

Here she stopped for a moment, lost in the
    reach of her thinking,
Which ran over the bounds of her speech in the
    stress of her spirit;
Soon again she came back to herself and spoke
    Greek unto Homer:
"Not alone the rise from the fall, thy beautiful
    Helen,

But the woman unfallen is also thy gift to us women —
She who never could lapse from herself in trial the sorest.
Now let me crown thy brow with this wreath for Penelope faithful,
For Arete, the mother, who dwells in the heart of her household,
For Nausicaa too, the maid of all maidens forever.
Take this gift from thy children, thou art the father of Hellas!
Which has been born to thy song and trained to the step of thy music,
Which will go singing thy strains down Time, in joy and in sorrow,
With the echo repeating itself in all nations, O Homer."

Thus spake Sappho, the soft-speaking Sappho, sweet Lesbian songstress,
Graceful she stepped, and loving she laid on his temples the garland,
Plucked by her hand and wove to a crown of the leaves of the laurel.
Echoing shouts of approval rang back from the hills and the sea-shore,
Even the wavelets, trying to walk, had come up to the bank-side,

Trying to talk had murmured afar their billowy
  answer.
Sweetly the rhythm she spoke, her spirit had
  caught it from Homer,
And the heroic hexameter yielded to lips of a
  woman,
Tamed by her gentle caress into lines of mel-
  lifluous movement,
Though it was used to the clangor and clash of
  the onset of battle.
Now the poet has heard in tenderest tones of the
  songstress,
Touched with Lesbian tints, the tune of his own
  mighty measure
Softened quite to the whisper of love in its deli-
  cate cadence,
Sung in praise of himself for singing the praises
  of woman,
Showing her highest worth, not sparing her blame-
  ful in error.
Fairest reward of the bard, when he harks to the
  heart of his verses
Beating out of a bosom that throbs in a joy to his
  music,
Flowing from lips that he loves, like a soft suc-
  cession of kisses.

But behold! another fair woman steps up to
  the front-line,

Forward she moves to that presence, it is the
  daughter of Homer,
Who in a gleam of her sunshine embraces the
  songstress of Lesbos,
And then speaks in low tones what her looks already are telling:
" Thou hast uttered the word of my heart to thy
  music, O Sappho,
Word which often has beaten the wall of my lips
  for delivrance,
Always in vain, for left to myself I never can
  say it;
But in the warmth of thy speech I can feel the
  hot beat of my bosom,
And that struggle of thine and of Helen's has
  sung me my battle.
Deep is the joy of my soul, and yet I have with
  it a trembling,
I have given myself all away, and yet I must
  keep me,
Sweet is every moment of life, and yet it is
  bitter.
What is this riddle of pleasure in pain and of
  pain in pleasure?
Would I might fly from myself, and yet to myself I would fly then.
. Tell me the great surrender which will restore me
  my freedom,
Speak it again, the magical word, the word of my
  weal now,

Overmaking me wholly in hope of the time of
    my ransom.
I would bathe in the stream of thy song as in
    waters of healing,
At thy voice my full heart which before had been
    closed, is open,
Like the flower which bursts at the breath of the
    spring from its bud-coat,
Still unwilling to show at first what is hid in its
    bosom."

What does this mystery mean which lurks in
    the speech of the maiden?
Not quite clear to herself is the meaning of what
    she has uttered;
Nearer the Lesbian songstress she drew, confid-
    ing in glances,
Then in a whisper she spake, the beautiful daugh-
    ter of Homer,
Clinging to Sappho, soft-speaking Sappho, the
    helper of love-pain:
" Tell me the story once more thou hast told so
    often already,
I can hear it again from thy lips and never grow
    weary,
I would hearken thy heart and live in the strains
    of its music;
Sappho, O Sappho, what is this love of the youth
    and the maiden,

Which thou singest in hundreds of songs to the
    sónorous cithern?"

Scarce had ended the speech when both were
    aware of another
Who had entered their thought and stood by
    himself in their presence;
Both looked hastily up, it was the fair youth
    of the Northland
Ready to speak, and his glances held the two
    women asunder,
Since the one of them blushed, and the other
    drew back in amazement;
Warm was his accent, though neither Ionic,
    Æolic, nor Doric;
Well he could say what he wanted and spake
    to the Lesbian songstress:
"Thou hast uttered the word of my heart to thy
    music, O Sappho;
I a stranger am here from afar, from the realm
    of the frost-gods,
Thy warm breath I have felt as it wafted in words
    from thy poems,
All the winter within me has melted, and I am
    the summer,
Tender summer of Hellas attuned to the lyre of
    Lesbos.
All the ice of the North to-day thou hast thawed
    from my bosom,

As thou toldest thy tale in the tale of the beauti-
    ful woman;
Helen I was myself, and I sank in the spell
    of her passion,
But I was also her spouse, to Troy I would
    march for my Helen;
Aye, the Greek I must win, or myself I shall
    lose forever."

  Here he stopped for a sigh, then passed to
    an undertone softly:
" What is this fearful joy, and yet an agony
    with it
Which allows no rest in the pain that is born
    of its pleasure?
Sweet is every moment of life, and yet it is bit-
    ter;
I had given myself all away, before I had known
    it;
Tell me the cause of this hungering lingering
    longing for something —
Sappho, O Sappho, what is this love of the youth
    and maiden,
Which thou singest in hundreds of songs to the
    sonorous cithern?"

  Smiling she touched the amorous chords with
    the tip of her finger,
Softly preluding the tones which turned into
    words in her answer:

"Both of you have the same pain, and both of
    you have the same pleasure,
Both of you sing the one song which runs to the
    very same ending;
Even the words of your lips I notice are pairing
    together,
Yes, young people, I think I can tell you concern-
    ing this matter,
Old is the tale to the old, yet ever is new to the
    youthful,
But to the poet it never can wear off the gleam
    of its freshness.
Much in myself I have studied the cause and the
    cure of this trouble;
What in longing is sighing asunder, the word
    brings together,
Hear me, then, both of you, daughter of Homer
    and son of the Northland:
Two are still twain and in pain, who were born
    to be one and one only.
Give me two hands — I shall join them to one in
    mine own at a heart-beat."

Sappho set down her sonorous shell, to the pair
    she drew nearer,
Till between them she stood and secretly reached
    out on both sides,
Took two hands in her own and laid them willing
    together,

Which of themselves, with a grip like Fate, were
    clasped in a promise,
While the eyes at each other shot fiery ratifica-
    tion.
Meantime the songstress was chanting a lay of
    the doings of Eros,
Singing for others she sang to relieve her own
    heart of its travail,
For the old wound, broken open, could only be
    stanched by the love-song.

Hark! the sound of a trumpet rolls over the
    hills in the distance!
What can it mean, interrupting this moment of
    joy by a startle?
There! once more it is rolling, it sends on its
    waves a light shudder.
Each let go the firm grip of the hand in the shock
    of the warning.

But the daughter has gone and whispered aside
    to her father;
What did she say to him there as she leaned to
    his ear with her blushes?
Joyful he was at the word and louder he spoke
    than a whisper:
"Happy I am — I have it foreseen — let me
    pledge you together;
Sorrowful too — ye both have to leave me be-
    hind — leave Hellas;

Still I feel you will take me along to the land of
    the future,
Aye, you will take our Hellas along and preserve
    it forever."

Louder, nearer, sterner, resounded the blast of
    the trumpet,
Bearing command it seemed and bidding to wait
    for the message;
Still no person appeared, but a ruler was surely
    behind it,
For authority spoke unworded in tones of the
    trumpet,
Strangely attuned to the roll of the thunder, the
    voice of the Heavens.

In response to the note of forewarning spake
    Homer prophetic:
" Nay, not yet, not yet — the tie is not yet to be
    fastened,
First this flame must be curbed and subdued to
    the oracle coming,
Else it will burn down the world, like Troy, in a
    grand conflagration;
No more Helens — one Helen is surely enough
    for all ages —
Bravely renounce the sweet thought, and prove
    yourselves worthy, renouncing;
Bravely renounce and renounce till the law hath
    declared its fulfillment."

Louder responded to Homer the blast of the ominous trumpet,
Louder, nearer it rolled and mingled its sound with his sentence.
As if giving the strength of its stroke to the words of the poet,
Who still added his warning to souls that might be impatient:
"Something else is announced, the best is to wait for the message;
It is near — the tramp can be heard — now wait for the message."

IX.

Polyhymnia.

The Psalmist of Israel.

ARGUMENT.

David, King of Israel, comes to visit Homer, having heard the songs of the Greek poet sung by Mesander, born in Cyprus, a Hellene and a representative of his race, the Hellenes (*pronounced as two syllables*) among Semitic peoples — Phœnicians and Hebrews. The two great poets sing for each other, and in their songs they give the Greek and the Hebrew views of the world. The poems of Homer and the psalms of David have just been written in the new alphabet of Phœnician letters; Typtodes and Mesander have copies of the two works. David and Homer sing several times, each recognizes the greatness and worth of the other. They become warm friends, as from Chios they look out upon the future to the westward. Hesperion and Praxilla are betrothed, and King David stays to take part in celebrating the marriage on the morrow.

Suddenly after the sound of the trumpet that
  rolled from the mountain
Followed a wave of deep voices of song that
  swayed to the sea-swell,
Choiring in tune to the strings of the harp and
  the tones of the timbrel,
Mid the clash of the cymbals and drum, and the
  clangor of cornets,
Loudly preluding new strains to be joined to the
  music of Hellas,
First to-day, where rises melodious Chios in
  billows,
Chios, the beautiful island, whose eye is the garden of Homer.
Slowly a caravan wound through sinuous turns
  of the mountain,

Shone as it rolled into vision out of the azure
 horizon;
Over the hilltops it heaved, it seemed to be hung
 from the heavens!
Gaily it glistened afar with the gleam of its gold
 and its purple;
Precious stones of the East, the onyx, the opal,
 the diamond,
Peeped with a thousand eyes from the front of
 the column advancing,
Peeped and sparkled and shot in a dance with the
 sunbeams of Chios.

"What high pomp of a monarch is that and
 where is he going?"
Each one asked of his neighbor, who gave no response to the question,
For he knew nothing to say, but stood and gazed
 in his wonder.
Statelier moved the procession while nearer it
 came, still nearer,
Till it had reached to the door where inside was
 sitting Homerus,
Sitting not far from the hearth by the altar he
 made for the Muses,
With his soul in a song he sat there and heard
 what was coming.

Royally rode forth a man, dismounted and
 stood at the entrance,

All the radiant train of his followers with him
    dismounted;
What a spangle of gems and twinkle of jewels
    like starlight!
Dark was the eye and crispy the hair and brown
    the complexion,
Strong was the curve of the nose of the King,
    like the beak of an eagle,
As it darts from its fastness of rock on the cow-
    ering rabbit.
Yet how soft lay his lip underneath the fierce
    hook of the nostrils
As if nought but compassion he knew, and could
    utter love only!
Merciful downward to earth and prayerful up-
    ward to heaven
Ran his glances, while under them glowed the fire
    of his daring.
In a lofty obeisance he raised up finger to fore-
    head,
Jeweled lightnings leaped from his hand to the
    eyes of beholders,
Making them blink in the flash, and answer the
    sport of the sparkles.
Then he murmured low tones of a something in
    syllables foreign,
To the man who stood at his side, and who
    seemed to be waiting,
Eager to let the fountain of speech gush up to
    the sunlight.

That was a different man from the rest of the
    men of the Monarch;
Not the same turn of the features he had, and not
    the same stature;
He was named Mesander — the versatile, clear-
    toned Mesander,
Knower of speech, reconciler of men, interpreter
    famous,
He was the tongue of the King who bade him tell
    of the journey.
Hark! he is speaking, now list to his voice! his
    words are Hellenic!
Thus he spoke in the rhythm and speech familiar
    to Homer:

" Hail to thee, poet, thou song of the West,
    and also its prophet!
Humbly we pray thee to give us to-day a glimpse
    of thy treasures,
And of our own we gladly shall grant what we
    can in requital.
This high Monarch has heard thy strains in the
    home of his people,
Over the roar of the seas, beyond Phœnician
    Sidon,
Where dwells Israel's seed in the holy land of
    Judea.
In his palace he listened with pain to the sorrows
    of Priam,
Deeply forefeeling in Troy and its fall the fate
    of his city,

Sacred Jerusalem, set on a hill by good Abraham's
    children.
Also he followed in hope the devious path of
    Ulysses,
In whose return he beheld the return of his peo-
    ple from bondage,
When they fled through the sea and the wilderness
    drear out of Egypt.
High beat the wish in his heart and rose to a
    longing resistless,
Thee to behold, the singer of Hellas — he too is
    a singer —
Ere the dark Fates of Death shall clutch thee and
    hale thee to Hades.
He has stepped down from his throne to pay
    thee a visit of honor,
Leaving his own far away, he has come to the
    country of Javan,
Turning the point of his law, which keeps him
    aloof from the stranger.
Greatest of musical Hellenes, thou, the voice of
    the Muses
Singing forever down time and making thy lan-
    guage eternal,
Homer, before thee stands Israel's sovereign,
    singer, King David."

 Such were the words of Mesander, the em-
    bassy's eloquent spokesman,
He in Cyprus was born, and long he had lived
    with Phœnicians,

Learning their manners and speech, when he
    came as sailor to Sidon;
Also he traded with Tyre, when Hiram was king
    of the country,
Hiram, the King of rich Tyre, the friend and
    ally of David.
Skillful in talking the tongues, Mesander had
    seen many nations,
Noting the merits of each, he spoke the language
    of concord,
Artful in dealing with men, he was often chosen
    as envoy,
Wandering over the world, as interpreter came
    he to Jewry,
Even a poet he was and doubly was dear to King
    David.
But he remained a good Greek, although he was
    born on the border,
Quite on the line where Shem and Japhet have
    fought for dominion
All through the ages, and mingled in battle the
    blood of their children.
Greek though he was, Mesander partook of them
    both in his spirit,
Sought to keep peace between the combative
    souls of the brothers,
Sought to make each understand the greatness
    and worth of the other,
Deftly uniting the East and the West in the
    truth that is common.

Good was the Greek and yet he was vain, the
    showy Mesander
Called by the envious Hebrew, although beloved
    by King David;
Vain of his gift he was, of his gift in the tongues
    and in song too.
How he would strut when he made a good speech,
    or perchance a good verselet!
He could put on more airs than David and Homer
    together.

When Mesander had spoken, the King looked
    around for a moment;
Lo! he is stopped in his look, he is caught in the
    glance of fair Sappho,
Tranced by her face and her figure he cried:
    "What a beautiful woman!
How would she like to appear in my palace, a
    daughter of Israel,
Aye, a wife to the King, and a light of Greek
    beauty to Hebrews!"
Sappho looked on the ground, she knew the lan-
    guage of glances,
Sappho knew the language of love, even when it
    is silent,
Though she did not understand the Hebrew, the
    language of David,
And Mesander kept still, for he honored the Les-
    bian songstress.

Then to the words of Israel's Monarch re-
    sponded Homerus,
"Welcome, O friend, to the isles of the sea, to
    the land of fair Hellas,
Enter my garden and home, to me thou shalt be
    as a brother!
Thy great name I have heard, it was borne from
    the realm of Phœnicians,
By the Tyrian princes who trade in their ships
    with Greek merchants.
Sweet though faint is the shred of thy song in the
    land of Achæans,
Floating over the sea from the East to the tune
    of the sunrise.
How I have longed to list to your Muses, so lofty,
    so holy!
Now the moment has come ere I pass into pitiless
    Hades;
Oft in my heart I have felt you had something I
    had not, but needed.
Strike the harp! sing the song! one burst of your
    heavenly music!
And of your God I would know through melo-
    dious lips of his servant,
For we all have need of the God, be he one, be
    he many,
Dwelling in man and the world, over Hellas en-
    throned or Judea.
Tell me the story of trials I heard concerning
    your people,

As from bondage it fled with its God from the
  land of the Nile-stream;
That, methinks, is the story of man, to be told
  him forever,
Oft repeating itself in his life and the life of the
  nations.
We the Greeks have also divinely been put under
  training,
Through sore trial our Gods have tested the love
  of their people,
Tested our mettle Hellenic to do the grand task
  of the ages;
Over to Troy we went and we fought ten years
  for our heirship,
Asia we had to assail that we save our beautiful
  Helen."

Then the dark king of the East laid off his garments of purple,
And a golden harp he took from the hand of its
  holder,
Harp of ten strings to which he chanted the
  praise of Jehovah.
Also his voice he essayed in a caroling upward
  and downward;
Sweet were the tones which he rapidly touched
  in the strains of his prelude,
Soft were the notes which he secretly hummed
  to himself for the trial,

Gently he glided to words, that wedded the
    tender vibrations,
Making the measures of song which skillful
    Mesander translated.
Homer hearkened, laying his soul to the lips of
    King David,
Who sang Israel's strain till it filled the fair
    garden of Chios:

"Happiest nation of nations I sing, whose
    God is Jehovah;
Blessed forever and ever the people whom He
    hath chosen,
Looking down from the heavens the children of
    men He beholdeth,
Israel's children He loves, but His law is the law
    of the nations.
Praise Him, my soul, the one holy God, He is the
    Almighty;
Praise Him, the King of the Kings, the Monarch
    of earth and of heaven,
Whose thoughts are a great deep, and His right-
    eousness like a great mountain;
Trust in the Lord and do good, for He laughs at
    the cunning of evil,
Its keen sword, when drawn against Him, shall
    pierce its own bosom.
He is the law of the world, which to men He has
    mightily given,

He is the law of the world, and He is also the
 judgment.
List to His voice as it speaketh aloud in the roll
 of the thunder,
See Him fold up the sea in His hand like a garment of waters,
Hark how the cedars of Lebanon crash in the
 breath of His anger!
Hark to His law, ye nations: No other God is
 before me."

In the might of his mood sang the King high
 strains of his language,
Which Mesander the spokesman turned to the
 speech of Homerus;
To the hexameter's swing he broke the wild
 cadence of Hebrew,
Tuning Israel's heavenly flight to the tread of a
 heathen,
Training in bounds of Greek measure the sweep
 of divine aspiration.
Oft he had done so before, and now he would
 peep in a scroll there,
Made of a papery rind of Egyptian reeds from
 the Nile fens,
Which he held in his hand, scratched over and
 over with scribblings,
Curious mystical signs which seemed to whisper
 in secret,

Only by him understood was the talk of those
  signs and their meaning,
Still their voice was not heard, for they talked in
  a flash to his eyesight.

But at last he raised up his eyes and folded his
  writing,
And in a glow he spoke, that Grecian of Cyprus,
  to Homer:
" Give him the roar of thy seas, as they rise like
  Icarian billows,
Give him the swell of thy heart as it heaves in
  the height of the battle,
Give him the roll of thy measures in waves of the
  blue Hellespontus ;
O Mæonides, sing him thy Zeus, the God of the
  Hellenes,
Father whose children are Gods who come with
  their help to us mortals.
Sands of the desert below, and glories of Heaven
  above us
He has sung — now give him thy concord of man
  and the world here,
Give him thy concert of Earth and Olympus,
  divine and the human,
And for thee I shall do what for him I have
  done — translate thee."

Softly Homer began with a prayer that fell
  into measures:

"Zeus, high father of Gods and of men, Olympian father!
Son thyself of old Cronus, consumer of all of his children,
Thou has escaped from his maw and dethroned thy pitiless parent,
Who would be all to himself in the world, without even offspring.
Hear me, O Zeus, me the mortal, but loving thy worship and order!
Not by thyself dost thou rule from the top of snowy Olympus,
Highest of all thy gifts thou dost share unto others — thy godhood,
Many divinities sit in a circle majestic around thee,
Gods and goddesses too are thy sons and thy beautiful daughters,
Whom thou hast raised to thy heights and with thee hast made to be rulers,
Ruling the air and the earth and even the underworld sunless,
Ruling the man in his deed and also his innermost spirit.
Still thou art ever the first among many, in mind and in power,
And in authority over the Gods thou art surely the sovereign,
Let any deity dare to question thy might for a moment,

Down to black Tartarus whirls he to sit with the
    hopeless Titans."

  Skillful Mesander now did his best to turn this
    to Hebrew,
Toning a word here and there to suit the fine ear
    of King David,
Fitting to music the thought, as it flowed from
    the heart of the singer;
But in spite of his skill, the translation ran rough
    in hard places.
Free Greek speech would not always dance to
    the tune of Semitic,
Homer's hexameters broke in the back at the
    gait of the psalm-song,
And the Monarch would scowl when he heard of
    the Gods in the plural,
Yet he would smile to himself at the noise about
    beautiful Helen,
For the God of the King must be one, though his
    wives may be many;
Gods of the Greek may be many, his wife is the
    one, the one only,
Whom to save he is ready to fight ten years with
    the Orient.

  Sly Typtodes had slipped up behind and
    peeped into the papers
Which the interpreter held in his hand when his
    reading had ended;

Then began to address him in whispers the pedagogue prying:
"What is that script which I see, that strange miraculous scribbling?
Have you too the mystical writ of symbols Phœnician?
Mighty it will be forever, preserving both David and Homer,
Rescued from sounds of the voice and fixed into signs for the vision.
And the schoolmaster now will have work in each new generation,
Teaching the name and the shape and the sound of the wonderful letters,
Till they together be put into words, the holders of all things.
Then the pupil will spell out the deed and the thought of aforetime,
Spurred by the sprig of the laurel held in the hand of the teacher.
That I call progress, that is the march of mankind to the better!
Nor will it stop till every youth in the land knows the letters,
Every youth in the world must know the Phœnicians symbols."

Ere Typtodes had done, strong currents had drowned out his whisper,

Strong loud currents of song that rose from the
    throat of the singer,
Overflowing all bounds of the sea when the tide
    runs the highest,
And it came from the fathomless heart of Israel's
    psalmist:
" Praised be Jehovah, in Him is our trust, the
    God of our Fathers,
From everlasting to everlasting He is the ruler!
In the land of Egypt we toiled and we wept in
    our sorrow,
Slaves were Jacob's children, but they were
    never forgotten,
From the slime of the Nile we fled to the shore
    of the Red Sea,
Always we saw a great hand reach out of the
    cloud round about us,
Smiting the chains of our bondage and pointing
    the way of our rescue.
Through the walls of the waters we crossed dry-
    shod on the bottom,
Long in the wilderness forward and backward in
    trial we wandered,
Till we returned to our home, the primitive home
    of our Fathers,
Bearing the law in our hearts, which was given in
    thunders at Sinai.
Sing, O my soul, the high song, the return to
    the land of our promise,

Sing it for me and for mine, and for wandering
   millions hereafter,
Millions on millions unborn, the countless sons of
   the future."

As he ended he turned to Hesperion, child of
   the Northland,
Into whose shadowy semblance he peered in a
   wonder while singing,
For that youth had the face among faces which
   look at the speaker,
Drawing him always secretly back to the spell of
   its gazes,
Back to itself it draws him, unconscious of magical
   power,
Showing him dreamlike glimpses of something
   afar that is coming.
Thus the youth of the North attracted the look
   of King David,
Who seemed glancing into futurity throned in
   that visage,
Far-off futurity throned in the visage of dreamful
   Hesperion,
As he stood there beside the beautiful daughter
   of Homer,
Who all the future had read in the soft blue eyes
   of the stranger,
Dreamful Hesperion, lately arrived from the
   snows of the Northland.

Soon the poet of Hellas began once more full
　of fervor,
Gently attuning his note somewhat to the music
　of David:
"Singer, thou art of the East, but thy strain
　belongs to the West too,
In it I hear the same voice that to me is the voice
　of the Muses,
By whose help I also have sung the return of my
　people,
That was the sad return of the haughty victori-
　ous Argives,
Coming from Troy in their ships to their homes
　on island and mainland;
Many were lost through wrath of the Gods, but
　the faithful were rescued,
Though the path was doubtful and long that lay
　on the waters.
Lately I finished the tale which tells the return of
　Ulysses,
Who on the passionate sea had to wander with
　foolish companions;
Much he endured in his heart, and much he
　doubted in spirit,
Till he came back to his Ithacan home, to Pene-
　lope prudent,
Where in peace he dwelt till the Fates had spun
　out his life-thread.
Great the return of Israel, hymning itself in all
　peoples,

Great the return of Achæa, which also will not
be forgotten.
Different may be our speech, but one at last is
the meaning,
Different may be our blood, but it all responds to
one heart-beat,
Different may be our Gods, but the Man is the
same in us both here."

Spoken the winged word, uprose divinely
Homerus,
Reaching out with his fingers, he felt for the
hand of King David,
Trip-hammer strokes of his heart beating time
to the voice of the Muses:
" Mortals may blame the Gods for their ill, but
it is their own folly,
Through themselves they must perish, ere Gods
are able to smite them,
Atè is sent for by man, else even the Gods could
not send her,
What through man the divinities do, is also his
doing,
His is the deed, though the world is divine in
which he can do it.
But the one deity truly is thine, the God of the
ages,
All shall pass away, but He abideth forever.
Hear my prophecy, hear it and weigh it, concerning two poets

Standing in Chios and looking afar on the worlds
    in the sunset;
One shall lift up the soul from below to the pres-
    ence immortal,
And will quicken the heart to worship, unseen,
    the Eternal;
But the other will show the trial and triumph of
    Heroes,
Singing into his strains the homage undying of
    beauty.
Both as brothers shall go down the echoing hall
    of the ages.
Echoing double one voice from the heart of
    Greece and Judea.
Two are the aisles in the temple of song, Hellenic,
    Hebraic,
One is the harmony under them both, the har-
    mony human,
Tuning to musical life the Man and the God in
    their struggle."

Slowly the poet of Hellas drew back to his seat
    in the settle,
But his mind ran on in its might, though his body
    was weary,
And he continued: "One thing more my spirit
    must tell thee,
Hear now my prayer, O David, and call it the
    prayer of Homer:

May the son ever be a much better man than his
  father!"

At the thought he suddenly turned and seemed
  to be looking,
Though he was blind, he seemed to be looking and
  prying about him:
"But I forget! I have a new pupil, where is he?
  Hesperion?
Where is Hesperion, dreamful youth of the neb-
  ulous Northland?
And I forget too my daughter, where is she?
  Praxilla? Praxilla?
Surely to-day she is roaming, my daughter, my
  sunny Praxilla!"

In a moment the crowd was moving and turning
  and looking,
All would peep at the pair whom the poet had
  coupled together;
What he had joined in his words, they surmised
  he had joined in his thoughts too,
Every boy in the school surmised what was going
  to happen,
Every boy in the school blushed red as if he were
  guilty,
Guilty of hiding away in his heart an arrow of
  Eros,
Which had pricked him with jealousy's pang,
  though slyly secreted.

First he peeped for his rival, but found no reward
　　for his peeping,
Saw no Hesperion, dreamful youth of the neb-
　　ulous Northland,
Then he would speak in low tones to his neigh-
　　bor, who had to make answer;
Each was disguising the timorous thought that
　　trembled within him,
Each was telling it too just through his careful
　　disguises;
Soon the whole school was a whisper, asking:
　　Where is Praxilla?
Soon the whole school was a whisper, replying,
　　Where is Hesperion?

Crabbed Typtodes, the schoolmaster, still
　　was present and looking,
But he nowhere saw what he looked for, the
　　daughter of Homer,
Whom he too would see and would sue in spite
　　of his wrinkles;
Teaching the verses of Homer, he weened he
　　could teach the fair daughter,
Writing Phœnician letters, he thought he would
　　write her a poem.
Vain is the effort, to-day he is wearied and
　　worried with waiting;
In his sandals he shuffles along to the side of
　　Mesander,

Whom he somehow thinks to be kin to himself
 in the spirit;
Him he bespeaks on a point quite aloof from the
 way of the lover:
" Long you have dwelt in Phœnicia, you say,
 and know all its learning;
Have you the songs set down in the signs of
 strange Alpha-Beta,
Cunning symbols of speech, that fix the fleet
 breath of the singer?"
"Yes," responded with joy the dexterous
 spokesman Mesander,
" All have been set down in signs so that we
 can hear them forever
Only by seeing them, look, the cunning Phœnician symbols!
Thousands of years from now, yea, millions on
 millions of ages,
Men will have but to look on these signs and will
 hear King David,
Magical signs of the word, which make the good
 poem eternal.
I have all of his songs scratched down on the
 folds of this scroll here."

Lowering still his tone, Typtodes spoke to Mesander,
Confidentially bending his head more near while
 speaking:

"I have noted it well; while you talked, I peeped
    over your shoulder.
But I must tell you a secret, which nobody knows
    of in Chios—
Long I have wrought to set down in these signs
    the poems of Homer;
What a task it has been—the burning by drops
    of my heart's blood!
It is done, but yesterday done, and to-day I have
    brought it,
Hid in my bosom; toilsome the work but I felt
    it was worthy,
Though I find fault with the failings of Homer
    and slash him to fragments;
See! I have poured out my life into writ, here
    it is, O Mesander—
One small roll out of many, the rest I shall fetch
    from the school-house,
One short day out of many, all which have sunk
    into Lethe."
  "Surely no idler thou art," said the Greek
    from the island of Cyprus,
And thou movest along with the world, the
    schoolmaster moves too,
Spirit needeth the letter, the letter too needeth
    the spirit,
Homer will last, but the pedagogue Chian will not
    be forgotten,
Who was the first to put into script the song of
    the poet,

Making him sing forever in spite of the Fates,
the grim spinners."

Both of the men had still something to say on
the matter of letters.
But they suddenly stopped when they heard the
voice of the poet
Not now chanting a musical strain to the Gods
and the Heroes,
But impatiently calling aloud, "Hesperion!
Praxilla!"
Twice he repeated, "Where is Hesperion! Where
is my daughter?"
"Here I am on this side," soon spake up the
youth of the Northland,
"Here I am on the other," responded the maiden
Praxilla.
Both of them spoke in their joy as they suddenly
sprang from an arbor,
Where they had hid from the crowd for a moment
of sweet conversation,
Words of the twain now blended together to
tenderest music,
And their voice was wedded in love, preluding
the marriage:
"For thy blessing we come, thy blessing, O
father Homerus."

Then both kneeled at his side, brave youth and
beautiful maiden.

"Rapid work, my children, too rapid, and yet
    I confirm it!
Who can catch and turn back in its flight the
    arrow of Eros?
Well I foresaw what was coming, I knew in
    advance the whole story.
Did you think because I was blind, I never could
    see you?
All the while I could see you doing just what I
    intended.
But enough! You have my approval, take now
    my blessing!"
Laying each hand on a head, he rose up with
    them together.

  Standing between the twain, once more spoke
    the poet to David:
"Thee I beseech, O Monarch, yet greater than
    Monarch, a Singer,
Stay with me here, for to-morrow is given in
    marriage my daughter;
Go to rest in my chamber and wake up renewed
    in the morning,
Both of us then shall sing together the song of
    the wedding,
Ere we send off the pair to the distant forests of
    Northland.
Thou must give them thy God, the One, and his
    high adoration,
I shall show them the Man, the beautiful Man in
    his freedom."

X.

Urania.

The Marriage.

ARGUMENT.

All come together in the morning for the wedding festival of Hesperion and Praxilla. The scholars have a choral dance in honor of the event; Glaucus and Demodocus confess their great disappointment. Sappho chants for the pair her last measures of love and good wishes. Typtodes brings as his bridal gift the poems of Homer written in the new alphabet. Homer and David give to the pair their blessing and with it their two books, which are to be borne to the new home, whither the happy couple now set forth on their journey.

Up rose the Sun in his car and lit the Ionian
 heavens,
Driving the timorous Dawn far over the sea to the
 westward,
Seeming to mount to the sky in flames that
 burst from his glances
For some joy that he felt and imparted to earth
 and to ocean.
Like a bridegroom he rose and put on his garments of splendor,
Gold he was strewing wherever he looked on the
 land and the water.
Warm was the thrill as he reached from afar
 with his radiant fingers,
Earth awoke at the touch and sprang up respond-
 ing in music,

Every creature was singing, even still voices of nature
Chanted the hymn of the Sun as he soared up the sky in the morning.
Purple and scarlet and gold were his regal changes of raiment,
Jewels he flung with his sheen in the lap of the beautiful island,
Which peeped forth from the waves in a smile at the sport of the sunbeams,
As from slumber it woke and lay on the bed of the billows.
Chios he kissed in a rapture, as if his bride he were kissing,
All the heart of the Sun was flowing to love and to marriage,
As he glowed and he glanced down into the garden of Homer.

Both of the poets had risen from sleep, the Greek and the Hebrew,
And were sitting together, in joy saluting the morning,
Which from earth and from heaven returned the high salutation.
"Beautiful is this world of Jehovah," shouted King David.
"Praised be his name, for his law is the law which endureth forever."

"Beautiful is this world of the Gods," responded
Homerus,
"Beautiful too is the man, divinely upbearing his
freedom."

Thus they continued their talk, which ran of
itself into measure,
All of their speech was a song, and each of them
sang to the other.
Two were the strains on the tongue, yet both
reached down to one key-note.
Skillful Mesander translated the twain and added
his comment.

Soon they all had gathered together with David
and Homer,
Hearing the note of the East and the West in the
words of the masters.
Lovely Sappho was present, the soft-speaking
songstress of Lesbos,
But she was silent, for eagerly now she heard the
new message,
Heard the voice of the law as it fell from the
lips of the psalmist,
Though she felt that the singer himself was not
free of its judgment.
Still in her thought she did not upbraid him who
rose after falling,
Nor condemn what her own tender heart had told
her was human.

Shifty Typtodes, the pedagogue Chian, doth
    seem to be absent ;
No, he is coming, yonder he shuffles along in his
    sandals,
He has set down the poems of Homer in symbols
    Phœnician,
Though he won not the daughter, he must be a
    guest at her marriage.
Look! he hastes up the path, and carries the
    rolls of his paper,
Rolls first made of the rind of the fen-born rush,
    the papyrus,
On which is written the word of the poet for
    ages hereafter ;
Book it is called, the scribbled peelings of rushes
    of Egypt.

    Next were seen the beautiful youths who sang
        in a chorus,
Gracefully stepping along, attuning their dance
    to the song-beat,
All the youths of the school were there arrayed
    for the wedding,
Spotless they shone in white raiment falling in
    folds to their motion.
From the East and the West they had come, all
    joined the procession,
And they began the high song with a festal pray-
    er together,

Prayer beseeching the presence divine of the
    God of Espousals:
"Hail Hymenæus, hail! O come to the island
    of Chios,
Come to the glorious island of song that is sing-
    ing thy praises!
Great is the need of thy presence to bless what
    is going to happen,
For the lots of marriage are now to be drawn by
    a maiden,
Rarest of maidens of Hellas, the beautiful daugh-
    ter of Homer.
Be not absent, O deity, rule the caprices of
    Fortune;
Hail Hymenæus, hail! make the tie of the pair
    everlasting!"

David the King drew near, and spake to the
    youth of the Northland,
" Speed thee afar to thy forests, and take this
    maiden Hellenic,
Her thou must win to thy love, for thou never
    canst marry a Jewess,
'Tis not allowed by the law — no hope thou canst
    have for my daughter,
Whom I have left behind with the rest of the
    daughters of Israel;
These we keep to ourselves for the glory and
    praise of Jehovah.

But unrewarded thou shalt not pass from my
 presence this morning,
All that is best of myself, whatever is good in
 my nation,
I shall give as a present to thee and thy people
 forever.
It shall attune thee anew to its song when thy
 soul is discordant,
From thy fall it shall lift thee on high with fresh
 aspiration,
It shall stead thee in trial the sorest, in death it
 shall stead thee.
Now its words have been written in signs that
 came from Phœnicia,
Musical sounds of the voice have been set down
 in signs for the vision
On that Ægyptian peel of a rush, called Byblus,
 the Bible.
We have brought it along on our journey —
 Where is it, Mesander?"

Here the translator suddenly stopped his talking Hellenic,
Spoke in Hebrew the word of reply which has
 not been translated.
Taking the folds of a curious roll written over
 with letters,
Looking the look of a victor, he handed it soon
 to the Monarch.

Meanwhile trembling in voice spake up good
  father Homerus,
" Now may life pass away, the end I have seen of
  my living;
When his work has been done, not long the
  mortal will tarry;
More cannot fall to my lot, my hours henceforth
  are a passage;
After to-day I shall sing no more, the spirit
  refuses;
Words cannot tell what I think, but bound the
  flight of my vision;
Life I have loved, for it was a deed, and it was a
  song too,
But it is done, and the time draws near — the
  time of my silence,
When the sound of my song will be but an echo
  repeating,
Ever repeating the voice which I flung on the
  breezes of Hellas.
Daughter, go; I send thee far off to the folk of
  the Northland,
Thither now bear my song, for it is my gift to
  the ages;
May thy children be heirs of the lay and the life
  of Greek Homer."

Such were the words of the parent, and they
  were never forgotten.

All of the company present were touched by the
    tone of the farewell,
For they seemed to hear the refrain of a lay in
    the distance,
Giving a soft response from beyond to the note
    of the poet,
Who was singing to-day the last, last strains of
    his swan-song.

Hark to the bardlings! a youth steps forth from
    the line of the chorus,
With a discord in look and in heart — it was
    high-born Glaucus,
Who from Lycia came, and now he sang to the
    maiden:
"I have tried to win the hand of the daughter
    of Homer;
How I longed to carry her off to the banks of
    the Xanthus,
Where is my sweet sunny home by the banks of
    the eddying Xanthus!
Honest my suit was to bear her away once more,
    the Greek Helen,
Peacefully bring back the beautiful prize of the
    world into Asia;
But I have lost, the Gods are against me, and
    turn from my people;
All I have lost, I must now see the bride borne
    off to the westward —

I the son of King Glaucus, and grandson of
    Glaucus the Hero,
I who am sprung far back of the seed of Bel-
    lerophontes —
Hail, Hymenæus, thy blessing upon the daugh-
    ter of Homer."

Scarce had he ended, when from the opposite
    side of the chorus
Stepped forth a youth of the West, in song and
    in love his great rival,
It was Demodocus, son of Demodocus, Ithacan
    rhapsode:
" I too sought for the hand of the beautiful
    daughter of Homer,
From this isle I would bear her away to the
    home of Ulysses,
Whence the old Greeks our fathers once came to
    the rescue of Helen.
Great was the deed they did, the deed of the
    Greeks, our fathers!
Beautiful Helen again I would rescue in fairest
    Praxilla,
Coming over the sea from my home to the
    island of Chios.
I have lost, let me go, I now shall become but a
    swineherd,
Son unworthy of men who took the citadel
    Trojan.

Hail, Hymenæus, thy blessing upon the daughter
    of Homer."

Forward came Sappho, the Lesbian songstress,
    the tenth among Muses,
Grace she revealed in her form and her speech,
    the fourth among Graces,
Aye tenth Muse of the Muses, and aye fourth
    Grace of the Graces,
As she sang to the pair mid the sweet low tones
    of her cithern:
  "Hail, Hymenæus, hail! make happy the
    bride and the bridegroom!
May the souls of the twain be one thought, the
    two lives be one living!
Make the marriage a presence, which they shall
    dwell in forever.
May the love of to-day be also the love of to-
    morrow!
You, O bride and bridegroom, you too I would
    move by my prayer;
When you come to your home far over the border
    of Hellas,
Sappho forget not, who was the first to join you
    together,
Making the love of your hearts to flow in the
    strains of her music,
Taking the hands of you both into hers and link-
    ing the promise.

Daughter of Homer and son of the Northland,
remember the songstress,
Sappho the Lesbian singing the love of the youth
and the maiden,
Hail, Hymenæus! make the bond of the lovers
eternal!"

Soon Typtodes stepped forth, in his hand were
the rolls of his writing,
Faithful he brought the work of his life as his
gift at the nuptials,
Though the beautiful daughter he won not with
all of his wooing.
But he hath his reward, his gift shall not be forgotten.
Gruffly with a grimace he muttered: Hail, Hymenæus!
Into the hand of the poet he put the magical
symbols.
Then he withdrew from the place — not the least
was the schoolmaster's present;
As he passed out of sight, he flung down a tear
on the gravel;
Once he looked back at his rolls, his life-task,
sad at the parting.

Then spake Homer, giving the pair his last benediction:
"Here, take my book, now writ by Typtodes in
letters Phœnician,

Keep it and let it still grow, one seed of your
    future existence,
Showing the beautiful world of the Gods which
    arose in our Hellas,
Showing what man must do with himself to build
    up a freeman."
  Then spake David, giving the pair his last benediction :
" Here, take my book, it too is written in letters
    Phœnician,
By some scribe — I know not his name — employed in my household :
Keep it and let it still grow, one seed of your
    future existence,
Showing the law of the world proclaimed in the
    land of Judea,
Showing the God, the one only God, and his
    worship in spirit."
  So to the Northland they took the two books
    of Homer and David,
Oldest and newest, twin books of all time, the
    Greek and the Hebrew,
Lovingly bore them afar to the West, the home
    of the nations,
Which shall kindle the light in their hearts and
    carry it further,
Where the two singers of Eld shall still sing daily
    their wisdom,
Voices resounding in millions of echoes from letters Phœnician,

Bringing their song to the present and handing it
  on to the future,
Ever renewing their strains in the soul that is
  ready to hear them,
Known far better hereafter than ever in Greece
  or Judea.
  Then the pair set out — Hesperion son of the
  Northland,
And Praxilla, fair maiden of Hellas, the daughter
  of Homer,
Quitting the garden where grew the orange, the
  fig and pomegranate,
Where the hills were a flutter of leaves of the
  silvery olive.
Soon they came to the shore, and there lay the
  boat of the bridal,
Covered with branches and leaves, and decked
  with the flowers of Chios.
Seamen raised up the mast and steadied it firmly
  with mainstays,
Then they spread out the sails to the wind and
  took the direction.
Oars they dipped in the brine, for trial made
  ready the rudder,
And the God sent a favoring breeze which blew
  from the island,
Yet a sigh mid the joy of the day it would
  whisper in snatches.
" Farewell forever, Praxilla my daughter! Farewell Hesperion!"

Light ran the ship as it cut with its keel
  through the billowy waters,
Laughingly sparkled the sea in the stroke of the
  vigorous oarsmen,
Over the rise and the fall of the ripples was rock-
  ing the vessel,
Muffled sang the great deep, upheaving and bearing its burden.
"Farewell forever, O Homer, my father! Farewell O Hellas."

From the shore all the youths of the school
  were gazing in sorrow,
Merrily still the vessel kept dancing away o'er
  the billow,
That was the last day of school, the end had
  come of their training;
Long they looked at the boat until it had vanished from vision,
Looked in the blue at the sail till lost in the haze
  to the westward,
Wondering whither it went and whether again
  they would see it.
When the small white speck of the ship had
  twinkled to nothing,
Longing the scholars turned for the sight and the
  speech of the poet,
But he was not to be seen, he had gone to his
  home with King David.
Soon they too had dispersed, each went his own
  way to his country.

Still the lovers sailed on far away from the gardens of Chios,
Onward they went in their joy, behind them leaving the islands,
Over the deep they sailed and came to the shore of the mainland.
Quitting the ship and the sea, they plunged into forest and desert,
Into the dangers of land far greater than perils of water,
Fleeting across the wintery border of beautiful Hellas,
Where it stretches beyond the abode of the Gods on Olympus,
To the regions where drinking their whey dwell the mare-milking Thracians,
Over the hills and the valleys away to the banks of a river,
To the stream that is bearing the flood of the wide-whirling Istros,
Still beyond and beyond, still over the plain and the mountain,
Over vast lands to the seas, and over the seas to the lands still,
Through the icicled forests, through the tracts of the frost-fields,
Still beyond and beyond, still over the earth and its circles,
Onward they passed, the daughter of Homer and son of the Northland —

Further and further they went, till they came to the homes of his people,
Bringing two books in their journey, the gifts of David and Homer,
Bringing two songs of the sunrise to sing to the lands of the sunset,
Songs still singing of God in his foresight and Man in his freedom,
Where the huge arms of the breakers are smiting the shores of the Ocean,
Ever beyond and beyond in the stretch of their strokes they are striking,
Striking the barrier of earth in the stress of their strong aspiration,
Beating, forever repeating, the strokes of the infinite Ocean.

www.ingramcontent.com/pod-product-compliance
Lightning Source LLC
Chambersburg PA
CBHW020816230426
43666CB00007B/1030